ARAB–LATIN AMERICAN RELATIONS

mo

ARAB–LATIN AMERICAN RELATIONS

Energy, Trade, and Investment

Edited by

FEHMY SADDY

Transaction Books
New Brunswick (U.S.A.) and London (U.K.)

© 1983 by Transaction, Inc.
New Brunswick, New Jersey 08903

Library of Congress Catalog Number: 83-440

ISBN: 0-87855-475-0 (cloth)

Printed in the United States of America

Library of Congress Cataloging in Publication Data
Main entry under title:

Arab-Latin American relations.

    Includes index.
    1. Latin America--Foreign economic relations--Arab countries--Addresses, essays, lectures. 2. Arab countries--Foreign economic relations--Latin America--Addresses, essays, lectures. I. Saddy, Fehmy, 1941-
HF1480.55.A65A7   1983   337.8017'4927   83-440
ISBN 0-87855-475-0

Contents

List of Tables

Acknowledgments

The idea of producing this volume grew out of the frequent contacts and stimulating discussions I have had with Georges D. Landau over many years. Working in the background from his base at the Inter-American Development Bank, Washington, D.C., he guided my steps in making invitations to the contributors from Latin America and in shouldering much of the task of making contacts and follow-ups. He fully shares with me the credit for producing this volume. Professors Abdul Aziz Said, The American University, and Irving Louis Horowitz, Rutgers University, gave me support and encouragement. Professor Nicholas Onuf, The American University, and Dr. Ronald McLauren, Abbott Associates, Alexandria, Virginia, read the introduction and made valuable comments. Professor Antun Harik, Beirut University College, shared with me some ideas on the subject of petrodollar recycling. Ms. Marinel Mobley's editorial and typing assistance made a qualitative difference. To all of them I owe much gratitude. The responsibility for any flaws in the materials contained in this volume rests with me and the contributors alone.

Preface

Arab–Latin American relations have grown in the last few years to an unprecedented level. The 1970s witnessed a phenomenal increase in diplomatic representation and economic exchange between Arab and Latin American countries. Cooperation between them within the framework of the United Nations has followed consistent patterns on most major political and economic issues. This cooperation strengthened the bargaining power of developing countries vis-à-vis industrialized ones and was instrumental in the initiation of the New International Economic Order. Trade between the Arab world and Latin America has risen at an extraordinary rate, to billions of dollars annually. Some Latin American countries have increased their economic activities in the Arab world by supplying food and manufactured products and undertaking construction and industrialization projects. For their part, some Arab oil producers with capital surplus have extended development aid and loans, or entered into joint ventures with banking institutions in Latin America. Thus Arab and Latin American countries have emerged as genuine partners in development.

This expansion in political and economic exchange has not received adequate attention in academic institutions or research centers and remains largely unexplored. Articles on bilateral economic relations between individual Arab and Latin American countries have appeared sporadically in periodicals addressed to the business community, but no concerted effort has been made to explore and evaluate the full range of cooperation between them. Coverage has been discontinuous, and Arab–Latin American relations as a whole have been investigated neither systematically nor in detail. One reason for this deficiency may be researchers' reluctance to engage in the analysis of a relationship that is still unfolding. Another reason may simply be lack of interest or awareness. Whatever the case, the responsibility for this deficiency rests with scholars and researchers in the Arab world and Latin America.

The purpose of the present volume is to compensate for this deficiency by providing an initial assessment of changes in Arab–Latin American relations in recent years and to project normatively some likely developments in the 1980s. Admittedly, this volume does not explore all aspects of these relations exhaustively, but focuses on some major areas in which Arab–Latin American relations have experienced a significant expansion. The sense of urgency to compose this anthology has made it necessary to focus on the more visible areas of cooperation and place less emphasis on areas which, while perhaps equally important, are less salient. The cultural dimension of Arab–Latin American relations has not been addressed except in passing, although this dimension is likely to play a much more important role in fostering these relations in the future. The political dimension has not been covered in the extensive manner it deserves, although references to political considerations permeate the individual articles. Instead, the focus of this anthology is on the economic factors that have provided a primary motive for the expansion of Arab–Latin American relations.

Since responsibility for exploring the various dimensions of Arab–Latin American relations rests primarily with Arabs and Latin Americans, a group of eminent and thoughtful officials, scholars, and consultants from both regions were invited to contribute articles for this anthology. Their background and experiences provide an impressive collection of talent and insight. Their essays reflect a unique composition in that some are quantitatively oriented, others normative, and still others more analytical in their approach.

The introduction to this volume attempts to provide a theoretical framework for Arab–Latin American relations. The concept of interdependence constitutes such a framework for the explanation and evaluation of these relations. Interdependence is analyzed in the context of the changing parameters of political and economic power in world politics which have stimulated the development of Arab–Latin American relations and which are likely to foster their growth.

Alejandro Orfila analyzes the new posture taken by Latin America in recent years and the role it has come to play in the Inter-American and international systems, with its renewed spirit of independence, equality, and enlightened self-interest. In this new environment, Latin America looks for cooperation with the Arab world for mutual development. He explains the role the Organization of American States can play in fostering political and economic relations between the two regions and calls for a dialogue that would establish them as "true partners in growth."

Abdullah H. Tariki outlines from personal experience the early cooperation between Venezuela and the Middle Eastern oil-producing countries to coordinate their oil policies vis-à-vis the multinational oil companies. He analyzes the circumstances that led to the formation of the Organization of Petroleum Exporting Countries (OPEC) and evaluates its activities. He addresses the question of oil revenues and their adverse effects on the oil-producing countries. He calls again for cooperation between Arab and Latin American oil producers to limit this negative impact and outlines a strategy for more advantageous arrangements that would serve both the Arab and Latin American countries.

Amaury Porto de Oliveira analyzes the oil requirements of developing countries within the general perspective of future world supply and demand of oil. He calls for circumventing the traditional strategy of industrialized countries by the evolution of South-South cooperation in energy matters, to meet both OPEC and developing countries' requirements for future development. He places particular responsibility on Arab and Latin American countries for devising initiatives in this direction.

Mohamad W. Khouja analyzes trade relations between Arab and Latin American countries and outlines their limitations and growth potential. Guided by the expansion of their trade relations in recent years, he proposes a number of measures to lessen limitations and encourage growth. Particularly important are the productive capacities of Latin American countries in food and industrial raw materials which may be exchanged for crude oil, fertilizers, and other petrochemical products from the Arab world.

Armando Prugue discusses the role of the Inter-American Development Bank (IDB) in financial cooperation between the Arab world and Latin America and its links with international financial markets. He proposes arrangements through which Arab investments in Latin American development projects could be undertaken with the supervision and guarantee of the IDB.

The editor calls for a new debate on "recycling" petrodollars in the 1980s. He reviews the arguments advanced in the first round of debate and evaluates them in light of the cumulative experience of the 1970s. He discusses the political, economic, and legal constraints evolved in the industrialized countries against OPEC's capital-surplus investments and presents the case in favor of increased investment in developing countries, particularly in Latin America.

Carlos Massad evaluates the growth of Latin American economies over the last two decades and demonstrates their strength and viability. However, he stresses the need for foreign investment if they are to continue to grow. He explores the economic advantages the Arab oil-producing countries would achieve by diversifying their portfolio of investments in real assets, giving relative importance to investments in Latin America. The importance of Massad's contribution is that it helps dispel the negative image of Latin America held by some Arab financial managers and articulates the economic basis for a strategy of investment diversification.

Francisco Orrego Vicuna focuses on political cooperation between Arab and Latin American countries in a broader international setting, taking as a case study their cooperation in the Law of the Sea conference. He demonstrates the effectiveness of this cooperation, together with other developing countries, to institute a more equitable order for the exploitation and sharing of sea resources.

Finally, Hussein Khallaf draws the comparison between Arab and Latin American countries in terms of economic structures, population, and cultural similarities, and concludes that the economic complementarity of both regions makes it advantageous for them to coordinate their economic programs and open their markets to each other. He calls for the initiation of a dialogue on a regional level to explore opportunities for cooperation and outlines a strategy for communication between concerned individuals, groups, and institutions in both regions in preparation for such a dialogue.

1
Arab–Latin American Relations in the 1980s: An Introduction

Fehmy Saddy

The 1970s planted the seeds of change which have come to dominate the view of the 1980s. Probably no other development was more important in recent history than the sudden rise to power of a number of Third World countries. World politics in the 1980s has become less Western centered, both politically and economically. Western hegemony has come into question and the relevance of Western civilization and lifestyle to other people and nations has been seriously challenged. Political analysts and social thinkers are speculating about the direction and shape of the new global political, economic, and cultural order.

The transformation of the international system has resulted in a greater measure of democracy and equality among states, regardless of whether such values have been enhanced or suppressed within these states. This transformation, in both real and perceptual terms, has rendered Third World countries more assertive vis-à-vis the traditional powers, thus enhancing Third World capabilities and freedom of action. One result of this process is the movement generated in the 1970s to restructure the world political and economic order and develop new patterns of interaction among states.

From the time the modern nation-state system was established after the peace of Westphalia in 1648 and until recent years, international relations were confined to the European powers. Their subject peoples in the Southern part of the globe were dealt with merely as surrogates. Even after becoming independent, developing countries in the South continued to depend on the North—often on their formal colonial overlords—for political and economic survival. Until the 1970s, this pattern prevailed in international relations, perpetuating a deep-seated political, economic, and cultural dependence.

The spirit of independence and self-assertion that prevailed in the 1970s highlighted the deficiencies of North-South relations and exposed their inadequacy in a world increasingly becoming both interdependent and decentralized. With the decline of Western monopoly of power and influence, North-South relations face a serious crisis of trust. While maintaining its relations with the North and pressing for the establishment of a more balanced program for survival for all,[1] the South has felt compelled to expand its relations horizontally, thus bypassing the traditional Western metropolis. South-South relations have become imperative in an interdependent world.

Dependency, Linkage, and Interdependence

In this evolving international environment, interdependence has been advanced as a theoretical framework to accommodate new patterns of interaction. After much controversy and debate in academic circles and policy centers during the last two decades, the Western world has come to admit that international relations can no longer be subjected to the analytical test of dependence and dominance.[2] This recognition has amounted to a fundamental change of perception born out of torment, pain, and soul-searching. For a long time the Western world refused to recognize that its relations with the Third World were characterized by interdependence because such admission would imply a recognition of its own decline. U.S. failure to achieve an "honorable" peace in Vietnam on its own terms underscored the limits of American political and military power. The ability of the Organization of Petroleum Exporting Countries (OPEC) to apply pressure on the industrialized world in terms of both the supply and price of oil undermined the Western claim of economic prosperity and political supremacy. In the span of only a few years, the United States and its Western allies lost much of their dominance in international political and economic matters. Gradually, hegemony began to share the global stage with the more conciliatory and pragmatic language of interdependence.[3].

Interdependence is not a concept that developed suddenly. Although it acquired popular currency only recently, interdependence is a synthesis of diverse concepts and theories that have paved the way for a broader understanding of the forces of change in world politics. Two theoretical frameworks, in particular, have provided the support for interdependence arguments. These are the dependency and linkage politics theories.

The concern of developing countries with political, social, and economic development over the past three decades has led them to conclude that political independence was meaningless as long as their economic dependence remained.[4] The failure of Western models of development in the Third World has been partially explained by reference to the external constraints on national development. For developing countries and their advocates in the West, dependency theory became the key to explaining the failure of development in the Third World.[5]

The counterpart to dependency theory is linkage politics theory, which made its formal debut in the 1960s.[6] The recognition of domestic constraints on foreign policy formulation and implementation, which linkage politics theory entails, is little different from dependency theory, which emphasizes external constraints on national development. The theory of linkage is another version of dependency in reverse. It embodies similar implications of constraints and highlights the same nuances, but it leaves out much of the Marxist rhetoric which dependency theory is often accused of employing.

Both theories gradually became inadequate to analyze the entire set of relations that evolved in the 1970s between and within nation-states. On the one hand, dependency theory seemed locked into a syndrome of dependence/dominance or center/periphery that excluded the possibility of symmetrical relations. It was not theoretically able to analyze relationships between peripheries, whether tied to the same or different centers. For example, it has become increasingly difficult in recent years to think of nation-states as either dependent or dominant. The configuration of world power has lost much of its traditional patterns: new centers of power in the peripheries, particularly in respect to certain important commodities such as oil, have emerged on the international scene, posing as much of an impediment to development as the traditional Western centers.

Linkage politics theory is not without problems, as time has shown. In particular, the line between the national and international systems has become increasingly blurred.[7] The lines of linkage politics could no longer be seen as emanating solely from the national context, but ever more intertwined with lines of influence emanating from other national contexts outside the boundaries of the political system. It has increasingly become clear, for example, that American foreign policy in the Middle East is as much influenced by the American domestic scene as by the domestic situation in Israel or Saudi Arabia. Therefore, in spite of the dynamism it has introduced in decision-making analysis, the inadequacy of linkage politics theory has become manifest.

The concept of interdependence which gained ground in the 1970s presents a more appropriate framework of analysis. It erased the static dichotomization of politics as domestic and international, and the characterization of relationships as dependent and dominant. The evolution and continued articulation of interdependence has been in keeping with new patterns of interaction and emerging power structures. Interdependence has become a central concept in the edifice of a New International Economic Order and has marked a new era of international relations.

While interdependence is often interpreted in economic terms to signify the increasing economic interdependence of nation-states, its underlying tone is political.[8] The dependence of the Western world on the resources of the developing world probably would not have been recognized if the former's access to the latter's resources had remained unchallenged. Economic interdependence is intimately tied to political interdependence. Interdependence has signified not only redressing the balance of power between the developed and developing worlds, but also the diffusion of political and economic power within the Western world itself. U.S. involvement in Vietnam raised questions in the Western world about the safety and wisdom of American leadership in the nuclear age. Driven by their self-interest and their own assessment of security, Western Europe and Japan have been drifting away from the United States. They have sometimes opted to chart their own paths in political and economic matters. Whether in oil policy, strategic defense, international trade, or the Soviet approach to Afghanistan and Poland, their perception of their interests and the policies they have adopted no longer lie in close association with those of the United States.[9]

This global diffusion of power has served to establish interdependence on stronger ground. As the global power equation is redrawn, developing countries in the 1980s are freer to act in their own interests. The declaration of a New International Economic Order[10] is inseparable from a perception of a new international political order. This new order reflects structural changes in the patterns of interaction among nation-states. The new orientation of developing countries to expand their relations horizontally is the product of a less hierarchical era in world politics and the result of political and economic interdependence.

The growth of Arab–Latin American relations falls within the framework of international interdependence. The diffusion of power in world politics has enabled both Arab and Latin American countries to become more independent in their relations and has rendered them freer to chart their own paths in international affairs. The imperative of dealing with the difficult economic problems which affected all countries in the 1970s forced Arab and Latin American countries to establish their relations on a permanent basis. More will be said later about the new elements that shape these relations in the 1980s. First, we shall outline their origins and limitations.

Origins and Limitations of Arab–Latin American Relations

Prior to World War II, Arab–Latin American relations were largely underdeveloped as most Arab countries were administered as territories under mandate by Britain and France according to the terms of the Treaty of Versailles in 1919. In the interwar period (1919-39), the only relationship between Arab and Latin American countries was derived from the presence of large communities of Arab immigrants in Latin America. Arab immigration had started in the mid-nineteenth century and intensified after World War I as many young men from the eastern Mediterranean region escaped conscription in the Ottoman army.[11] During the mandate period, Arab immigrants, mostly Syrians and Lebanese, maintained their links with their countries of origin through the French embassies in Latin America.

After the independence of Syria and Lebanon in 1945, there was little incentive for them, and much less for other Arab countries, to expand their relations with Latin American countries beyond the establishment of a few embassies and consulates to serve their communities of immigrants. There were a number of reasons for this attitude. First, Latin American countries were perceived in the Arab world as far off lands not easily accessible by sea or air and, like Arab countries, largely underdeveloped and unstable. At a time when proper communication was lacking, the Arab mind, fed by the tales of Arab immigrants who lived in the deep countryside, conjured up images of Latin America that consisted of jungles, wild beasts, and disorder. Such images have changed in recent years, but a residual remains entrenched in the minds of many Arabs, even today.

Second, in the postindependence period, the Arab countries looked for the West to help them build their political and economic systems and were in no mood to turn their attention to other underdeveloped countries with conditions similar to their own. They were committed to the Western model of development, even when some of them started to experiment with socialism. Latin America was perceived as a source of raw materials and, like them, a region in need of Western technology and capital for development. The idea that Latin America has very limited trade or technology benefits to offer the Arab world is still held by some Arab economists today.

Third, this negative perception of Latin America was fostered by the circumstances that surrounded the creation of Israel in 1948. With the exception of Cuba, Latin American countries overwhelmingly support-ed—against the strong opposition of the Arab countries—the UN General Assembly resolution that called for the partition of Palestine.[12] The historical accounts of the UN deliberations reveal the extent to which Latin American votes were instrumental in making the Jewish aspiration to statehood a reality,[13] even while such support was not always a deliberate and conscious choice. Until the mid-1950s, when a large bloc of newly independent countries was admitted to membership in the United Nations, the United States dominated the General Assembly largely through its influence over Latin America. In the vote for partition of Palestine, the United States exerted unprecedented pressure on some of these countries and others to reverse their earlier position, thus ensuring the passage of the resolution.[14] The Arab countries retained, for many years, a resentment toward Latin America based on the continuing and ongoing tragedy of Palestine.

In the years that followed, Latin American support for Israel con-tinued unabated while Arab interaction with that part of the Western Hemisphere remained insignificant. Only Cuba and Venezuela main-tained good relations with the Arab world. The Arab countries main-tained good relations with Cuba, both before and after the 1959 rev-olution. The need for coordination in oil matters resulted in close coop-eration with Venezuela, especially after the formation of OPEC in 1960. The Latin American countries had not felt the need to develop better relations with the Arab world and persisted in their strong support of Israel. The source of this support is partially the sympathy that exists in Latin America for the Jewish people and their state. But the support is mostly the result of conscious policies of the United States and Israel in Latin America.

The traditional hegemony of the United States over Latin American countries ensured their continued support for its policy in the Middle East. This policy remained strongly pro-Israeli until the mid-1970s when consideration of Arab oil started to force a certain measure of change. The United States helped Israel establish good relations with most Latin American countries through various inter-American organizations.[15] It facilitated Israeli–Latin American technical cooperation programs within the framework of the Organization of American States (OAS).[16] Israel established a reputation for expertise in agriculture, irrigation, land development, and cooperatives, and was willing to put this expertise at the disposal of Latin American countries.[17] It became a nonregional member in the Inter-American Development Bank (IBD) and sought to become an active partner in the development of Latin America. Israel's attempt to maintain a high profile and draw the sympathy and support of Latin American countries has been enhanced by wealthy, articulate, and politically active Jewish communities in Latin America.

It could have been expected that Arab immigrants in Latin America might have played at least a moderating role in Latin American foreign policy toward the Arab/Israeli conflict, balancing off the influence of Jewish communities. Yet this has not been the case until recent years. Although Arab communities are larger and more prosperous, they are politically aloof. They have consistently identified with their new countries of residence where they engage in lucrative business. Coming from humble social and educational backgrounds and rising to riches in their adopted countries, they were not unlike other immigrants who tend to develop a conservative "immigrant" mentality and see in their new homes unquestioned virtues and none of the vices that characterize their countries of origin. Arab immigrants in Latin America have been relatively uninformed and politically naive. They are often critical of Arab governments for one reason or other. They are strewn with petty rivalries over their claimed social status. Whenever they identify with their countries of origin they invariably refer to the city or village from whence they came, and they have established societies and clubs to glorify and perpetuate their parochialism.[18] However in recent years, Latin Americans of Arab descent have begun to show more interest in Middle East politics.[19] This newly active segment of the Arab community tends to be well educated and politically conscious. It represents the middle class and is less visible in the social activities of the Arab communities than the earlier generation of immigrants.

It might also be expected that the common cultural characteristics shared by Arabs and Latin Americans should have played an important role in fostering their relations. Among advocates of stronger Arab–Latin American relations, there are those who believe that these relations are motivated, or at least facilitated, by this shared culture developed many centuries ago in the Iberian Peninsula.[20] The mingling of blood that took place over the span of seven centuries (711-1492) produced a unique culture manifested today in its basic characteristics in both the Arab world and Latin America.[21] Even if one minimizes the influence of this common heritage, the argument goes, it is difficult to overlook the influence Arab immigrants have had on the political, economic, and cultural life of Latin American countries. The argument is valid, but only half true. There is no denying that some shared cultural traits exist in the Arab world and Latin America. The Arabized Spanish and Portuguese, or the Mozarabs, did contribute to the colonization of Latin America and did shape its socioeconomic development.[22] This process continued in modern times after the influx of waves of Arab immigrants to Latin America. Cultural similarities could also play an important role in fostering relations between the two regions. However, the cultural argument leaves out some important variables in the formation of the Latin American culture.[23] The demographic composition of Latin America today is complex and strikingly different from that of the Arab world. The flow of European immigrants to Latin America since the early nineteenth century has come to alter the culture of the original inhabitants and early settlers. That Latin America today is Catholic in religion and Western in outlook suggests many implications in terms of philosophy, self-image, and perspective. Any similarities between the Arab and Latin American cultures are only in part a legacy of common heritage; they are largely the shared characteristics of underdevelopment. The influence of the mosque in the Arab world and the church in Latin America may have produced similar perceptions and attitudes, but the subtle differences they generate in each culture make for qualitative and fundamental differences.

Recent Development of Arab–Latin American Relations

Arab–Latin American relations began to experience some change at the beginning of the 1970s. This change was the result of conscious efforts on the part of some Arab countries to alter their policies toward Latin America. These efforts were in turn assisted by the global transformation that began to take shape in the 1970s, which placed the Middle East at the center stage of international political and economic developments. The growth of Arab–Latin American relations has been shaped by their cooperation at the United Nations and other international forums, together with African and Asian nations, to bring about the New International Economic Order. Today these relations are a function of their perceived interests in the framework of their economic interdependence.

In 1972 some Arab countries launched a diplomatic offensive prior to the 1973 Arab/Israeli war. Saudi Arabia, Egypt, Syria, and Lebanon sent their foreign ministers on tours to Latin American countries to gain their support for the withdrawal of Israel from the occupied Arab territories in fulfillment of UN Security Council Resolution 242 of November 2, 1967.[24] The diplomatic offensive was carried out in Western Europe and in various Asian and African countries as well. The Arab countries did not place much hope in the possibility of bringing the Latin American countries over to their side, but they were hoping to capitalize on the gains they were making in Africa, in particular, to attract the attention of Latin American countries to their cause.[25] The diplomatic offensive produced only marginal results in Latin America, and the Israeli position in the continent remained firm. Although the influence of the United States over Latin American countries began to wane, in the Middle East it continued to ensure most Latin American votes in the United Nations, where Arab demands were presented regularly but without conclusive results.[26]

The 1973 Arab/Israeli war and the subsequent oil embargo reversed the image of the Arabs in Latin America as well as in other parts of the world. The Arab states may have lost the military battle with Israel, but they emerged politically victorious.[27] They proved to be capable of fighting a war and, henceforth, gained respect. The challenge they presented by their oil embargo to countries that supported Israel, and the financial aid they provided to countries that supported them, made them look more credible as foes or friends. The oil embargo also produced rippling waves throughout the Western world, and Latin American countries began to experience gradually the negative effects of the embargo through their economic relations with the United States and Western Europe.

The Arab world has been identified with the Third World since the establishment of the nonaligned movement at the Bandung Conference of 1955, where President Nasser of Egypt, together with President Tito of Yugoslavia and Premier Nehru of India, was among its prominent leaders. The Arab countries were also the driving force behind the "Group of 77." They formed an important bloc in international meetings where their position was continuously strenghtened by the growing number of developing countries which joined the group in later years. Troubled in their relations with Western countries, particularly the United States, over the Palestine question, they have often found themselves standing in opposition to these countries on international political and economic matters as well. In a sense, they have represented the voice of dissension in an international system traditionally operated from Western capitals. Their outspoken positions against imperialism and exploitation and their calls for more balanced international economic relations gradually gathered support from other developing countries. However, the Group of 77 lacked the power to enforce its positions, and for many years simply simmered in its frustration. The breakthrough in the dialogue between the Group of 77 and the industrialized countries over matters related to international development had to wait until 1974 to receive any serious attention, as a result of the challenge posed to Western interests by the Arab oil embargo.

The significance of the Arab oil embargo is that it enabled other developing countries to identify with the challenge it posed and to gain self-esteem and psychological power. After the embargo was imposed, OPEC instituted a fourfold increase in the price of oil without prior consultation with the major oil companies. Once both steps were successfully accomplished, the process of restructuring power in the international system began. The Arab members of OPEC, in particular, increased their power by their majority in the organization and by amassing substantial financial assets. The Arab world was again at the center stage of international politics. It was not only an area where the Arab/Israeli conflict threatened world peace and security, but was also a major source of much-needed oil, a large market for the export of agricultural and manufactured commodities, and a source of highly prized surplus capital funds.

Until the mid-1970s when the serious drive toward the establishment of a New International Economic Order began, Latin American countries, except Cuba, could be described as passive participants in the Third World movement. None of the Latin American countries participated in the formation of the nonaligned movement at Bandung, and even in 1973, when the movement held its meeting in Algeria, only a handful of them took any part in it, and mostly as observers.

The gradual identification of Latin American countries with the Third World movement, and particularly with the political and economic positions of its Arab component, was a result of a new perception of their national interests. This new perception was largely shaped by the deteriorating relations between Latin American countries and the United States. These relations had always been uneasy, but they started to run into difficulties in the early 1970s.[28] The "destabilization" of democratically-elected President Salvador Allende of Chile in 1973 proved to many Latin American countries that U.S. advocacy of democracy in the continent was not without qualifications bearing upon its imperialistic interests. Throughout his tenure as the architect of U.S. foreign policy from 1968 to 1976, Henry Kissinger showed only a limited interest in Latin America at a time when the region was facing mounting economic problems and social unrest.[29] Consequently, even the military regimes that have traditionally had intimate relations with the United States began to defer to popular pressure, motivated by pragmatic considerations of their own survival.

Latin American countries have had many outstanding economic problems with the United States. These extended over the issues of bilateral and multilateral aid, export of their products to the U.S. market, terms of foreign investments, and the operation of multinational corporations in their territories. In addition, Latin American countries have extended coastlines and some depend on their sea resources for food. The invasion of their maritime economic zones by technologically advanced American fishing fleets continued to be a sore spot in their relations.[30] Negotiations over these issues were pursued for years without conclusive results. Gradually Latin American countries began to feel that little could be gained by persisting in their commitment to a "partnership" that was becoming increasingly difficult. The indissoluble "Catholic marriage" in which they had entered with the United States after World War II at the formation of the Organization of American States (OAS) became less attractive in comparison with the "marriages of convenience" they could conclude in the larger bargaining setting at the United Nations.

It was at this historical moment that Latin American countries began to show a genuine interest in the Third World movement, which raised in international forums issues of direct interest in them, such as the conduct and operations of MNCs, exploitation of sea resources, foreign investments, and the terms of international trade and transfer of technology. Latin American countries began to see the benefits they could derive from a closer association with the Third World movement.[31] But not until they decided to support this movement more openly could they foresee the prospect of solving their outstanding problems with the United States within larger international bargaining settings.

A significant product of this new identification with the Third World movement has been the closing of ranks between Arab and Latin American, together with Asian and African, countries. The coordination of their positions became effective in the various forums that have constituted the components of the New International Economic Order, such as the Conference on International Economic Cooperation,[32] the Law of the Sea Conference, the various UN conferences on trade and development, and the nonaligned conferences. It was almost unthinkable in the early 1970s that so many Latin American countries would attend any type of activity in Cuba.[33] Yet by the end of the decade they joined the larger community of developing countries.

Interdependence and Arab–Latin American Relations in the 1980s

The steady expansion of Arab–Latin American relations since the mid-1970s has been directly related to recognition of their common interests in an increasingly interdependent world. Leading Latin American countries have found it necessary to come to terms with Arab political demands. Arab countries also noticed the new independent role major Latin American countries began to play in world politics and the benefits they could derive from their support at the United Nations. Venezuela had to cooperate with Arab members of OPEC over the pricing of oil and other energy related matters. Although not an OPEC member, Mexico too had to maintain close relations with Arab oil producers. Luis Echeverría, former president of Mexico, championed the cause of the Third World, of which the Arab countries constitute an important part.[34] Brazil depends on the Middle East for its oil imports and could hardly remain indifferent toward Arab political demands. Other Latin American countries adopted more even-handed positions regarding the Arab/Israeli conflict. When in 1975 the UN General Assembly was called upon to vote on a resolution equating Zionism with racism, the votes of the Latin American countries showed an almost total reversal of a pattern that had remained consistent for some three decades.[35]

The sudden elevation to prominence of a number of Arab oil producers also placed them in a position of international responsibility. Their control of oil resources forced them to come into contact with countries which had previously dealt with the major oil companies. Many Latin American countries had little reason to develop interest in small and far-away lands in the Middle East, but soon discovered they could no longer remain aloof from them. The successive increases of oil prices left oil-importing Latin American countries with balance-of-payment deficits, which they sought to reduce by borrowing from the Special Facility of the International Monetary Fund (IMF) and other funds made available to them by the World Bank. These facilities have been financed by major contributions from OPEC, particularly its Arab members.[36] OPEC established its own Fund in 1976 to help developing countries meet the cost of their oil bills.[37] In addition, various Arab development funds were established to finance projects in developing countries.[38] These funds have been open to Latin American countries.

Some newly industrialized Latin American countries, such as Brazil and Argentina, for example, have realized that they could offset their trade deficits with the Arab oil producing countries by increasing their exports to the Arab region. They have sought to open the Arab market to their commodities and attract Arab capital for investment. A detailed inventory of economic relations between Arab and Latin American countries within two years of the oil price increase in 1973-74 shows a phenomenal expansion.[39] This upward trend of economic exchange has since continued unrelented, bringing the volume of trade between the Arab world and Latin America to unprecedented levels.[40] This trend has been matched by a similar increase in diplomatic exchange and the beginning of a movement to initiate an Arab–Latin American dialogue.[41]

Arab–Latin American relations have been progressing without the benefit of notice, much less a theoretical framework. The growth of these relations represents a case of South-South relations that has become imperative in the 1980s.[42] On normative grounds, exclusively vertical North-South relations would unavoidably result in the perpetuation of underdevelopment in countries of the South, and ensure their further exploitation by the North. Exploitation is regarded here as a function of the disparities in power, productivity, and organization between the interacting parties. The futility of bringing relations between developed and developing countries to a balanced position calls for a shift in their relations. Arab, Latin American, and other developing countries would greatly benefit from intensifying their interaction within a strategy of self-reliance. Their similar economic and social conditions and comparable levels of development make the "sharing" of developmental experiences more rewarding than the "transfer" of such experiences from industrialized countries. By identifying the complementary aspects of their economies, they could develop a mutually beneficial system of cooperation. In such a system, exploitation is unlikely to take place on the scale experienced by developing countries in their relations with the industrialized world. Their mutual benefits from a balanced exchange would serve as a stimulus for further growth and development.

This volume attempts to explore the boundaries of interdependence in Arab–Latin American relations in broad terms. The essays included in this anthology, whether quantitative, normative, or analytical, draw the outline of an unfolding interdependent relationship that is largely economic. However, the political and cultural dimensions of this relationship are present and should gain stronger ground as Arab–Latin American relations proceed. This functional approach is positive-oriented and views cooperation as an upward movement. The experience of other regions and countries in cooperation shows that interaction may also breed conflicts of interest. At this stage in Arab–Latin American relations this may be premature. The initial signals indicate that positive thinking is justified.

Notes

1. *North-South: A Programme for Survival.* Report of the Independent Commission on International Development Issues under the chairmanship of Willy Brandt (London: Pan Books, 1980).
2. See particularly Karl W. Deutsch and Alexander Eckstein, "National Interdependence and the Decline of the International Economic Sector, 1880-1957," *World Politics* 13 (1961): 267-99; Karl W. Deutsch, Chester I. Bliss, and Alexander Eckstein, "Population, Sovereignty, and the Share of

Foreign Trade,'' *Economic Development and Cultural Change* 10 (1962): 353-66; Karl W. Deutsch and Bruce M. Russett, "International Trade and Political Interdependence," *American Behavioral Scientist* 6 (1963):18-20; Kenneth N. Waltz, "The Myth of National Interdependence," in *The International Corporation*, ed. Charles P. Kindleberger (Cambridge, Mass.: MIT Press, 1970), pp. 205-23; Richard N. Cooper, "Economic Interdependence and Foreign Policy in the Seventies," *World Politics* 24 (1972):159-81; Richard Rosecrance and Arthur Stein, "Interdependence: Myth or Reality?" *World Politics* 26 (1973):1-27; Peter J. Katzenstein, "International Interdependence: Some Long Term Trends and Recent Changes," *International Organization* 29 (1975):1021-34.

3. In the 1960s, models of bipolarity, multipolarity, and bloc system were fashionable. "See Karl W. Deutsch and J. David Singer, "Multipolar Power Systems and International Stability," *World Politics* 16 (1964):390-406; Wolfran Hanrieder, "The International System: Bipolar or Multibloc?" *Journal of Conflict Resolution* 9 (1965):299-308; Kenneth Waltz, "International Structure, National Force, and the Balance of World Power," *Journal of International Affairs* 21 (1967):215-31; Richard N. Rosenau, "Bipolarity, Multipolarity, and the Future," *Journal of Conflict Resolution* 10 (1966):314-27; Roger D. Masters, "A Multi-bloc Model of the International System," *American Political Science Review* 55 (1961):708-98.

4. See Johan Galtung, "A Structured Theory of Imperialism," *Journal of Peace Research* 8 (1971):81-117.

5. The literature on dependency theory is too large to be included here. Among the classic treatments of this theory see in particular André Gunder Frank, *Capitalism and Underdevelopment in Latin America* (New York: Monthly Review Press, 1967); Paul M. Sweezy and Paul A. Baran, *Monopoly Capital: An Essay on the American Economic and Social Order* (New York: Monthly Review Press, 1966); Harry Magdoff, *The Age of Imperialism: The Economics of U.S. Foreign Policy* (New York: Monthly Review Press, 1969); Immanuel Wallerstein, *The Modern World System: Capital Agriculture and the Origins of the European World Economy in the Sixteenth Century* (New York: Academic Press, 1974); Suzanne Bodenheimer, "Dependency and Imperialism: The Roots of Latin American Underdevelopment," *Politics and Society* 1 (1971):327-57; Celso Furtado, *Obstacles to Development in Latin America* (New York: Anchor Books, 1970).

6. James N. Rosenau (ed.), *Linkage Politics: Essays on the Convergence of National and International Systems* (New York: Free Press, 1969).

7. Harlan Cleveland, "The Internationalization of Domestic Affairs," *Annals* 442 (March 1979):125-37.

8. Fehmy Saddy, "A New World Economic Order: The Limits of Accommodation," *International Journal* 34 (Winter 1979):16-38.

9. For the differences between the United States and its Western allies over the reaction to the Soviet invasion of Afghanistan, see *International Herald Tribune*, January 18, 1980. For the differences between the United States and West Germany over the reaction to the military takeover in Poland, see *Newsweek*, January 18, 1982, p. 40.

10. The declaration was passed by the U.N. General Assembly during its 6th special session (April 9–May 2, 1974).

11. Michael M. Hall, "The Origins of Mass Immigration in Brasil, 1871-1914."

Ph.D. dissertation, Columbia University, 1969; Jose Francisco Carneiro, *Immigração Colonizção no Brasil* (Rio de Janeiro: Publicação Avulsa, 1950).

12. Regina Sharif, "Latin America and the Arab–Israeli Conflict," *Journal Of Palestine Studies* 1 (Autumn 1977):98-122.

13. Fred Khouri, *The Arab-Israeli Dilemma* (Syracuse: Syracuse University Press, 1971), ch. 3.

14. Khouri describes the pressure that was applied in this telling paragraph: "The United States and the Zionists led the lobbying efforts of the pro-partition forces. The delegates, as well as the home governments of Haiti, Liberia, Ethiopia, China, the Philippines, and Greece were swamped with telegrams, telephone calls, letters, and visitation from many sources, including the White House, Congressmen, other government officials, and prominent persons from a number of business corporations and other fields of endeavors. These assured the two-thirds vote required for the partition resolution." Ibid., p. 55. Of the thirty-three states that voted for the partition of Palestine, twelve were Latin American (Bolivia, Brazil, Chile, Costa Rica, Dominican Republic, Ecuador, Guatemala, Nicaragua, Panama, Peru, Uruguay, and Venezuela). Argentina, Colombia, El Salvador, Haiti, Honduras, and Mexico abstained. Cuba voted against the resolution and Paraguay was absent.

15. *Deadline Data on World Affairs,* Inter-American Relations (Greenwich, Conn.: DMS Inc.) p. 24.

16. Ibid., p. 246.

17. Edy Kaufman, Yoram Shapira, and Joel Barromi, *Israel–Latin American Relations* (New Brunswick, N.J.: Transaction, 1979), pp. 42-48.

18. Ibid.

19. In 1974 the First Arab–Pan American Congress was held in Buenos Aires, Argentina and established an Arab–Pan American Federation (Fearab-Pan-americana) of Arab communities in Latin America. The congress meets annually in a different country. It met in Washington, D.C., in 1981.

20. This theme runs through official statements and joint communiqués of Arab and Latin American leaders on official visits.

21. Nicholas J. Debbané, *L'Influence arabe dans la formation historique, la littérature et la civilization du peuple brésilien* (Cairo, 1911); Gilberto Freiyre, *The Masters and The Slaves: A Study of the Development of Brazilian Civilization* (New York: Knopf, 1956); Adelino Brendao, "Influencias arabes na cultura popular e no folclore do Brasil," *Revista Brasileira de Folclore* 11 (1971):65-84.

22. See H.V. Livermore (ed.), *Portugal and Brazil: An Introduction* (Oxford: Clarendon, 1953).

23. See Charles E. Griffin (ed.), *Concerning Latin American Culture* (New York: Columbia University Press, 1940).

24. *Arab Report and Record,* May 16-31, 1972, p. 249; June 1-15, 1972, p. 273; August 1-15, 1972, pp. 373, 384; August 16-31, 1972, p. 395.

25. These efforts are reviewed by Kaufman, ch. 3.

26. Although Latin American countries often differed from the United States in their voting behavior at the United Nations, they remained relatively consistent with the U.S. vote on the Arab/Israeli conflict. See Joel Barromi, "Latin America and Israel," *Middle East Review* 3-4 (1975):38-41.

27. Both Egypt and Syria scored initial military successes during the 1973 war, but they had to withdraw later from most of the positions they had occupied. The Third Egyptian Army was encircled by the Israelis, which forced Egypt to ask for a cease-fire. The impact of the initial military successes, however, was psychological, because they symbolized a sense of redemption.

28. These relations were analyzed in a report by Sol Linowitz, *The Americas in a Changing World* (New York: Center for Inter-American Relations, 1975). A recent report by the Aspen Institute for Humanistic Studies analyzes the changing relationship between the United States and Latin American countries and calls for new approaches and policies in the 1980s. *Governance in the Western Hemisphere: A Call for Action* (New York: Aspen Institute for Humanistic Studies, 1982).

29. Lewis H. Diuguid, "OAS Begins 11-Day Meeting," *Washington Post*, May 9, 1975, p. 26.

30. The Latin American countries were the first to advocate the 200-mile Economic Zone. For an illuminating discussion of this and related matters at the Law of the Sea Conference, see chapter 9 in this volume.

31. R.H. Hellman and H.J. Rosenbaum (eds.), *Latin America: The Search for a New International Role* (Beverly Hills, Calif.: Sage, 1975).

32. The conference was chaired by Gumersindo Rodrígues of Venezuela.

33. Out of the then twenty-four Latin American countries, the following twelve attended the meeting: Cuba, São Tomé and Principe, Argentina, Bolivia, Granada, Guyana, Jamaica, Mauritius, Nicaragua, Panama, Peru, and Trindad and Tobago. These countries represent different shades of political ideologies. *Newsweek*, September 17, 1979, p. 14.

34. Presient Luis Echeverría of Mexico was hoping to replace Kurt Waldheim as UN secretary general when his turn in office was to run out. The support of the Arab bloc at the UN would have been essential for his candidacy.

35. On the analysis of the Latin American voting patterns on the Arab/Israeli conflict and their reversal in 1975, see Sharif, particularly Tables 2-4.

36. In 1980 OAPEC (Organization of Arab Petroleum Exporting Countries) members contributed $6.8 billion, or 2.34 percent of their GNP to development assistance of other developing countries, in comparison with 0.37 percent of the GNP of OECD (Organization for Economic Cooperation and Development) countries. *World Development Report 1981*, Table 16, pp. 164-65.

37. On the operations of the OPEC Special Fund, see *IMF Survey*, August 6, 1979, p. 242.

38. On the operations of these funds, see *IMF Survey*, February 5, 1979, p. 37, and August 20, 1979, pp. 349-50.

39. Fehmy Saddy, "The Emergence of New Arab–Latin American Relations: A Case of Cooperation among Developing Nations," Ph.D. Dissertation, The American University, 1976.

40. "Latin America and Middle East Draw Closer," *Latin American Weekly Report*, December 7, 1979, pp. 68-69.

41. See the report of OAS secretary general Alejandro Orfila on his visit to the Middle East in March 1977. OEA/Ser. 4, CP/doc. 708/77, May 17, 1977.

42. A meeting for South-South Dialogue was held in India in early 1982 as part of the Global Negotiations under the auspices of the United Nations. See *Washington Post*, February 25, 1982.

2
Latin America and the Arab World: A New Dialogue

Alejandro Orfila

In the contemporary world the Latin American and Caribbean states are not only regional powers but—consistently with their long diplomatic experience in international affairs—major world actors. At the same time a new element has been introduced into the traditional regional relationship: Latin America and the United States are now acting as equals and coparticipants in the international system.

This transformation in regional outlook and arrangements has occurred without much fanfare. However, two U.S. scholars, Abraham Lowenthal and Albert Fishlow, have assessed this change in an essay for the Foreign Policy Association. They believe that Washington should respond to Latin America's emergence by joining with other hemispheric powers to build a more equitable and effective international order, from which both the United States and other nations would benefit.

Traditionally, the key goal of the American family of nations has been regional interdependence. After they broke their bonds with the Old World, our nations have dreamed and fought for the establishment of new and more perfect forms of regional coexistence. This central aspect of American international life must be kept in mind in any considerations about the Western Hemisphere.

During the present century the Americans have not only shared an historic vision of regional interdependence, but they have learned to translate this into new and well-defined realities, including:

- The Inter-American system and the Organization of American States, a model for all countries aspiring to live in peace.
- The search for regional economic integration, which has led to the establishment of several regional and subregional economic groupings: in Central America, the Caribbean, the Andean region, and the Latin American Integration Association.

- An increasing number of joint transnational projects in manufacturing, mining, energy, the production of agricultural items,
and their marketing. These integrative trends are reflected especially in the generation and distribution of electricity and the physical
integration of border areas taking place in many sectors, including
water and flood control, river transportation, telecommunications,
education, and planning.

The basis for evolving a common regional policy founded on a
modernized special relationship among the OAS members—and rooted
in a coequal arrangement of mature partners—is quite clear. The basis
remains the common principles, traditions, and ideals agreed to by
hemispheric nations, as reflected in the legal instruments of the inter-
American system and the broad-gauged Charter of the Organization of
American States. Within this framework, Latin American countries are
moving toward establishing a new international order, grounded on the
new dynamics of a transformed regional relationship. The Western
Hemisphere currently offers a unique opportunity for mankind to
accelerate the pace of world development by forging a policy of regional
improvement as a foundation for global cooperation and development
because:

- The American region has the world's largest share of untapped
material, energy, and agricultural resources. It also possesses the advanced technologies essential to building modern industrial nations.
- The region has a long tradition of comparative international peace
among countries with secure—if still somewhat undeveloped—transportation lanes in all parts.
- The area's largely middle-income societies should grow at a faster
rate over the next twenty-five years than other nations—both advanced and developing. The foundations for accelerated development
are generally in place.
- A common system of values and traditions in the region is being
forged. Already the United States is the fifth largest Spanish-speak-
ing nation in the world.

Yet to focus on regional development is in no way to move away from
other regions, be they Europe, Africa, Asia, or the Middle East. Today,
absolute self-sufficiency is impossible for the Western Hemisphere or
any region. Today all nations are an integral part of the world system.
Isolationism is not passé, it is inconceivable. To seek greater improvement does not mean pursuing regional isolation. No society today, no
matter how wealthy or powerful, is capable of existing outside the

international community of nations. The real greatness of each country and region hinges upon its contribution to the common international good.

Latin America and the Arab World

What is true for the American region is equally true for the Arab world. Both areas are seeking to strengthen their regional capacities so that they might more effectively participate in the world system. Both Latin America and the Arab world face many similar or related problems and needs. However, each region has different resources and experiences which may be interchanged to complement one another's development. This provides a unique opportunity and challenge for cooperation.

Both Latin America and the Arab world enjoy rapidly expanding economies, and they both need to expand even more because of their growing populations and employment requirements. Increased trade is of primary importance for these two areas for the development of their economies. Latin American countries must have a more rapid growth of exports to meet their heavy debt burden, to purchase the necessary imports, and to help finance their development. On the other hand, the Arab countries need trade to provide them with essential raw materials for their burgeoning industries, and with food and other consumer goods necessary for their growing populations.

The Arab countries have capital resources which must be invested in a way that will yield payments for the financing of their development, even after their petroleum reserves are depleted. Also, their food requirements are immense and, due to the rapid increase of population as well as the aridity of their lands, it is clear that they will need to continue importing great quantities of food for years to come.

It seems logical that at least part of the Arab oil-exporting countries' surplus revenues should be channeled to the development of agriculture, not only in that part of the world, but also in Latin America where the potential in this sector is enormous. Considering the 122 million hectares of arable land in Latin America of which only approximately 9 million are presently under cultivation, there still remain 113 million hectares ready to be exploited if only the financial resources were available. Investment in agriculture would be doubly beneficial to the Arab countries, not only to satisfy their food requirements, but also to help them acquire the Latin American experience in such fields as the production of coffee, livestock and poultry breeding, and irrigation.

As middle-income countries, Latin American states possess a strong capital-absorptive capacity. At the same time they are able to produce the kind of commodities and manufactured goods which can be integrated into the Arab consumer market. While Latin America's capital-absorptive capacity is enormous, its capacity to attract public international funding is diminishing. Why is this so? Precisely because these countries are now viewed as middle-level countries and international lending agencies are giving priority to assisting the less developed Fourth World countries. Thus Latin America is hard-pressed to find financing for its much-needed infrastructural development—roads, ports, transportation, and communications.

In the energy sector lies another opportunity for horizontal cooperation and complementary exchange. The Arab countries are pursuing a policy of exchanging petroleum for technology—a policy which could benefit Latin America, relying almost solely on petroleum as its source of energy for the expansion of its ever-growing industries. Latin America possesses intermediate technologies which could be exchanged with the Arab countries for their petroleum. This exchange could cover such diverse fields as fishing, nuclear and solar energy, as well as food processing, rural credit, and community education.

Education and training is a very important activity in any economy, not only for the development of human resources to fuel the economic growth desired by governments, but also to fulfill individual human needs of self-fulfillment, employment, and a decent standard of living. This sector receives priority attention in most countries of both regions. This is especially demonstrated by the oil countries' granting of thousands of scholarships for their nationals to study around the world. Latin America has a long and rich experience in formal education, as well as in developing appropriate mechanisms for nonformal and technical-industrial systems to provide training opportunities in nontraditional areas of economic activity. Transfer of technology in industry, science, and education would be most appropriate between these two regions of the world, because much of this may be applied and adapted to the Arab world, especially in countries undergoing the establishment of new industries.

Role of the OAS

Founded in 1948 as the successor to the Pan American Union, the Organization of American States (OAS) is the world's oldest multilateral regional body for international cooperation. Through it, the twenty-eight member states seek to maintain peaceful relations and enrich the quality of life of their peoples by furthering their economic, social, and cultural development. The following major organs carry out the work of the organization:

- The General Assembly
- The consultation meeting of ministers of foreign affairs
- Three councils: the Permanent Council, the Inter-American Economic and Social Council (CIES), and the Inter-American Council for Education, Science, and Culture (CIECC)
- The Inter-American Juridical Committee
- The Inter-American Commission on Human Rights
- The General Secretariat
- Specialized conferences
- Specialized organizations

The OAS and its organs cooperate with intergovernmental, semi-official, and nongovernmental organizations that pursue similar goals. Its programs are financed by a regular budget to which all member states are required to contribute according to an established scale of quotas, and by special multilateral funds, to which member states make voluntary contributions.

Supplementing the activities carried out with the organization's own budget, the General Secretariat cooperates with nonmember states and international and private agencies to provide increased services to member countries. Within this sphere fall the efforts to promote the OAS/Arab dialogue.

In March-April 1977, as OAS secretary general I visited several Arab countries (Egypt, Jordan, Kuwait, Saudi Arabia, and the United Arab Emirates) to make a preliminary inquiry into the possibility of initiating cooperation with those countries. Egypt became a Permanent Observer to the OAS in May 1977, and has already launched programs in agricultural and rural development in cooperation with the OAS.

The visit I made to the League of Arab States was followed by a resolution on March 29, 1977 by the league calling upon its member states to consolidate and strengthen Arab-Latin American friendship and cooperation. More recently, the executive secretary for education, science, and culture made a formal visit to the secretary general of the Arab League to discuss the possibilities of cultural exchange and cooperation for development through the organization's programs.

The OAS has a long history of expertise in training and human resource development in virtually all development fields whereby multilateral cooperation would be possible through its various programs. There are also several specialized agencies of the OAS which could assist in this complementary role: the Pan American Health Organization, the Inter-American Children's Institute, the Inter-American Commission of Women, the Pan American Institute of Geography and History, the Inter-American Indian Institute, the Inter-American Institute of Agricultural Sciences, the Inter-American Defense Board, the Inter-American Statistical Institute, the Special Consultative Committee on Security, and the Inter-American Nuclear Energy Commission. The Arab countries should find the Latin American model of regionalism and regional integration of great interest.

Working together Latin America and the Arab world can become true partners in growth, a partnership which would signify an invaluable exchange in which similar as well as complementary needs of their different countries and of the region as a whole would be satisfied.

3
Arab–Latin American Cooperation In the Energy Field

Abdullah H. Tariki

The concept of cooperation among oil-producing and exporting countries to protect their interests against the monopolies of European and American oil companies was first conceived by the government of Venezuela. In 1948 a Venezuelan delegation visited the Middle East to discuss the concept of cooperation and exchange of information. The prevailing thought among the authorities visited by the delegation was that it was attempting to poison their relations with the oil companies. This initial negative reaction was to change in light of later developments in the oil industry and the behavior of oil companies themselves. This chapter will trace these developments which ultimately led to the establishment of the Organization of Petroleum Exporting Countries (OPEC), with the active support of Venezuela, and will assess Arab-Latin American cooperation in the energy field.

Genesis of the Concept of OPEC

Prior to 1950, oil revenues constituted a marginal source of revenue for the governments of oil-exporting countries in the Arabian Gulf. The governments of these countries at that time received only four English shillings for each ton (six cents per barrel) of oil exported. In the early forties the production of oil in this region was limited because the oil discoveries made in the thirties were closed down in 1939 when World War II broke out.

In the aftermath of the war developmental activities commenced in the oil fields of the Arabian Gulf. In the late forties, Arab and Iranian oil began to compete with Venezuelan oil in Western Europe and the United States. This fact possibly prompted the Venezuelan government to dispatch a delegation to the region to explain the conditions underlying the oil concession agreements in Venezuela. In 1943, the Venezuelan government enacted a law under which oil concessionaires were obliged to pay the Venezuelan government through different income taxes no less than half of the total profits of the oil companies through their operations in exploration, production, and export of crude oil and petroleum products. This was known at that time as the fifty/fifty profit-sharing formula. However, this formula was not exact, for the Venezuelan government was receiving income from the oil companies in excess of 50 percent. Further, the stiff competition for oil concessions in Venezuela obliged the oil companies to grant the government advance payments, or an increase in royalties from 12.5 percent (in kind or cash) to 18 percent or even higher in some instances.

Venezuela was considered by Middle Eastern oil producers as a model to be emulated. While Venezuela subjected the oil companies to income tax, they were exempted from this tax in the Middle East countries. In the late forties these countries began to demand equal treatment with Venezuela. It must be remembered that oil concessions in the region commenced with the concession in Iran in 1902, and were followed by concessions in Iraq, Kuwait, Saudi Arabia, Qatar, and the rest of the Arab emirates.

Acting on behalf of Saudi Arabia as oil minister and upon my return from a trip to the United States in 1948, I provided my superiors with memoranda advising them that the oil concession agreements in Saudi Arabia be amended to fall in line with those in Venezuela. I pointed out that despite the stringent conditions of Venezuelan concessions, they did not impede it from becoming the biggest oil exporter in the world.

The oil companies began to appreciate Saudi demands and were able to convince the U.S. government of their legitimacy. The U.S. ambassador to Saudi Arabia asked his government to accept the Saudi viewpoint. Negotiations between the Saudi Arabian government and Aramco started in late 1950 and were successfully completed in December of the same year, reaching an agreement retroactive to January 1, 1950. Under this agreement, Aramco would be subjected to income taxes, provided that the government took royalty and income taxes equal to the net profit of Aramco, or that total government take from income taxes and royalties did not exceed Aramco's take from the project. However, this agreement contained many deceptive elements. For example, it considered royalties or the share of the owner of the land (in this case the government), as a portion of the income tax, while conventionally royalties were considered a portion of the general expenses in the United States and Venezuela.

A Trip to Venezuela

In reading the oil trade literature, it came to my attention that a national petroleum congress was to convene in Venezuela in August 1951. I decided to invite myself to the congress, and for that purpose I contacted the executives of Aramco to assist me in obtaining a visa. There were no diplomatic relations between Saudi Arabia and Venezuela at the time, and the Saudi government had failed to invite the Venezuelan delegation which visited the area in 1948 to explain the Venezuelan oil concessions.

The late Cy Hardy succeeded in obtaining a visa for me from the Venezuelan Embassy in Washington, and I was able to attend the first Venezuelan National Oil Congress. I was welcomed at the congress by Venezuelan graduates from the University of Texas whom I had known and by other graduates I did not know. I was overtaken by their generosity and felt they were interested in developing cooperative arrangements in oil matters between Venezuela and Middle Eastern oil producers.

Despite the fact that I had not been officially invited to the congress, I was able to attend the meetings and listen to the discussions. It was explained to me that the reason I had not been officially invited to the congress was because of the absence of diplomatic relations between Saudi Arabia and Venezuela. Added to this fact, many Venezuelan officers and some civilians had apparently very cordial relations with the oil companies and were sensitive to anything that might affect these relationships.

The Venezuelan government was liberal in granting oil concessions to the oil companies and was receiving large revenues which were spent superfluously on consumer commodities imported largely from the United States. The joke at that time was that Venezuela imported everything from the United States, including eggs.

The Venezuelan press was excited about the presence of delegations from the Middle East at the congress. Official delegations which attended the congress were from Egypt and Iran. The Venezuelan press carried a coverage of their activities including interviews and welcomed the opportunity to meet them. Their presence, it was stated, signaled the beginning of cooperation among oil exporters for their mutual interests which, in turn, would protect them from exploitation by the international oil companies.

My stay in Venezuela afforded me the opportunity to visit the oil fields in the eastern and western parts of the country. I was also able to compare the treatment workers received in Venezuela with that in Saudi Arabia. Venezuelan oil workers had a union which negotiated their contracts with the oil companies specifying work conditions, while the oil workers in Saudi Arabia lived under hard conditions and received very little pay. I decided to bring this matter to the attention of the Saudi government since the production cost of Saudi oil was low compared to that of Venezuela, although it is of better quality in terms of gravity and sulphur content. I departed from Venezuela with the conviction that a return visit was necessary to foster relations between the peoples of the oil-exporting countries.

On the way back I detoured to Baghdad and Tehran. In these two capitals I discussed my experience in Venezuela with Iraqi and Iranian officials and emphasized the need to create an environment of cooperation among us and the government of Venezuela. All of us suffered from the tyranny of the oil companies which interpreted the oil concession agreements in their own interests and at the same time harmed the interests of the peoples of the oil-exporting countries. I also emphasized the substantial experience Venezuela had accumulated in its relations with the oil companies and the fact that it had achieved better terms with them. Officials in Iraq agreed with my assessment. Officials in Iran, while more conservative, encouraged me to continue my efforts in this direction. The chairman of the National Iranian Oil Company referred me to one of his staff members who spoke fluent Arabic. The latter was Amir Abbas Hoveyda who later became prime minister during the reign of Shah Mohammed Reza Pahlavi. Mr. Hoveyda was responsive and encouraged me to continue my drive to create an atmosphere of cooperation and exchange of information among the oil-producing countries.

During my stay in Venezuela, I learned from my Venezuelan friends about the Democratic Action party which in 1943 had passed the laws that forced the foreign oil companies to pay income taxes to the government. It was also brought to my attention that the succession of dictators in Venezuela had forced the leaders of this party to go into exile to Europe, the United States, and Mexico. I learned of the efforts of the minister of hydrocarbons and mines, Juan Pablo Pérez Alfonso, who was the driving force behind these gigantic achievements. I was looking forward to the day when I would meet this imaginative Venezuelan. With the fall of the dictatorship in Venezuela in the late fifties and the return to democracy, the Democratic Action party returned to power. Pérez Alfonso assumed the portfolio of minister of hydrocarbons and mines in the new government.

The First Arab Petroleum Congress

The first Arab Petroleum Congress was held in Cairo in 1959. The governments of Venezuela and Iran were invited to send delegations as observers. Venezuela sent a large delegation comprising two ministers, deputies from the Venezuelan parliament, technicians, and representatives of the press. The head of the delegation was no other than Juan Pablo Pérez Alfonso. I was highly impressed with his strong personality, his dedication and loyalty, and his readiness to cooperate in our mutual interest. The presence of the Venezuelan delegation lent seriousness and international status to the deliberations of the congress. Since 1951 I had been looking forward to meeting Pérez Alfonzo to gain from his experience in dealing with the international oil companies whose only interest was to maximize their profits, even if this was done at the expense of other countries' natural resources.

The proceedings of the first Arab Petroleum Congress moved smoothly. There was considerable interest in the congress by oil-consuming countries and the foreign oil companies which tabled numerous studies. An exhibit of equipment used in the oil business was held in Al-Jazira Exhibition Center in Cairo, which was visited by President Gamal Abdel Nasser. The president was excited about popular interest in oil and considered the general awareness of oil matters a promising sign. He viewed oil as the strongest economic and military weapon in the Arab arsenal, and a platform around which Arab potential could be brought together. He also thought oil surpluses could spearhead joint Arab projects.

The deliberations of the first Arab Petroleum Congress lasted one week. The heads of the Arab delegations and their guests were anxious to seize this opportunity to come out of the congress with agreements on several issues. The most important of these was to stop the international oil companies from playing with the price of oil at will, such as reducing or increasing prices without consultation with host governments. The oil companies considered posting oil prices as their own prerogative and that host governments had no right to interfere. Just prior to convening the congress, the international oil companies reduced oil prices and justified this action by claiming that oil supply exceeded demand and hence it was necessary to lower prices in order to sell the surplus oil.

The discussions in the congress were candid and, in addition to informative papers, others dealt with policy positions. Delegates from Iran, Venezuela, Saudi Arabia, Iraq, Qatar, Kuwait, and the Arab League found it necessary to have a closed meeting to draw a plan which would protect their governments from the hegemony of the international oil companies, help them conserve oil resources, and ensure just oil prices. The closed meeting was attended by the director of oil affairs in the Arab League, the head of the Venezuelan delegation Pérez Alfonso, the head of the Iranian delegation, the Kuwaiti representative, the Iraqi delegation, and myself as representative of Saudi Arabia. It was agreed in this first meeting that secret side meetings would continue until an agreement was reached. Such an agreement would then be presented to the respective governments so that necessary steps could be taken in the event the oil companies continued to manipulate oil prices without prior consultation. The drafted memorandum stated that the oil-producing countries would cooperate and consult on all matters pertaining to relations with the oil companies operating in their countries. It was also agreed to call for an extraordinary meeting in the event that the oil companies reduced oil prices without prior consultation.

The first Arab Petroleum Congress achieved a basic framework of cooperation among oil-exporting countries and was a success from our viewpoint. The concept of establishing an international center for oil cooperation to serve the countries that largely depended on oil exports for their revenues became deeply rooted in the minds of the Arab delegates and others that attended the congress.

Creation of OPEC

Shortly following the end of the first Arab Petroleum Congress, the international oil companies reduced oil prices for the second time without prior consultation with the governments concerned. This was considered a frontal challenge to sovereign independent states, namely the oil-producing countries. The action taken by the oil companies embarrassed the governments of these countries, particularly as it followed publication of the decisions of the first Arab Petroleum Congress. This left no choice for these governments but to implement the decisions of the congress. The delegates who signed the secret memorandum called for a meeting. All the delegates were extremely anxious to make it clear that they were not ready to be brow-beaten by the oil companies and were ready to face the challenge. Oil prices were felt to be the prerogative of sovereign countries, and the foreign oil companies had no right to ignore the sovereignity of independent states. Cables were exchanged, and in my capacity as director of oil and mineral affairs of the Kingdom of Saudi Arabia, I received a cable from Pérez Alfonso reminding me of the secret meeting in Al-Maadi, Cairo, and requesting that an urgent meeting be held to discuss the matter. I also received a cable from Sheik Jaber Al-Ahmad Al-Jaber, minister of finance of Kuwait (the present amir) asking for no leniency and demanding implementation of the secret decisions taken in Al-Maadi. I presented these cables to the then crown prince and prime minister the late King Faisal, who was also minister of finance and national economy. He showed a keen interest in taking appropriate steps against the challenge of the oil companies. Prince Faisal advised that the meeting be held outside of Saudi Arabia, since Riyadh at that time did not have the facilities for such a large meeting. I obtained his permission to travel to Kuwait, Iraq, and Iran to discuss with the authorities the date and place of the meeting. In Iraq it was decided, after convincing Brigadier Abdul-Karim Qasim, then leader of the Iraqi Revolution, that the revolutionary government of Iraq would call for a meeting in Baghdad on August 10, 1960 and extend invitations to all governments whose delegates had signed the secret memorandum in Cairo. The governments of Iran, Kuwait, and Venezuela accepted the invitation, and Qatar agreed to send a delegation to observe the meeting. At this meeting it was agreed to establish the Organization of Oil Exporting Countries (OPEC). The first decision made by OPEC was to reinstate oil prices to levels prior to their reduction by the international oil companies following the first Arab Petroleum Congress. The oil companies ignored this decision and did not recognize OPEC as a body representing the oil-producing countries. Whenever the necessity arose to meet the secretary general of OPEC, the oil companies made it clear that they were not meeting him in that capacity but simply as a representative of his own government.

The international oil companies refused OPEC governments' request to reinstate oil prices to their levels prior to the last reduction and managed to freeze them from 1960 to 1970. At the same time, prices of all other commodities imported by oil-producing countries from oil-consuming countries were rising at an annual average of 7 percent. To meet the increased import prices, OPEC members reverted to increasing oil production, and this in turn increased oil supplies in the international market. This situation created an imbalance between supply and demand which led to a slump in oil prices resulting in a decline in real revenues from oil.

OPEC: Enlarged and Expanded

The international oil companies did not welcome the birth of OPEC. In fact, they did not recognize it and ignored its existence. In case they were obliged to have a dialogue with OPEC, they emphasized that they were dealing with its officials as representatives of their own governments with whom they were bound to negotiate under the terms of the oil concession agreements. The industrialized countries met the establishment of OPEC with a cool reception. The Swiss government refused to extend to OPEC's headquarters in Geneva diplomatic privileges normally accorded to international organizations. This prompted OPEC to move its headquarters to Vienna.

OPEC is an international organization created to protect the interests of its members against the industrialized countries and to help other developing countries, which export other raw materials, to follow in its footsteps. The development of this organization may be divided into three stages.

First Stage: 1960–65

During this period the organization strove to achieve recognition by the foreign oil companies, affiliated with the industrialized countries that imported and consumed large quantitites of oil, such as the United States, the United Kingdom, France, Japan, and the rest of the noncommunist countries of Europe. These countries took OPEC lightly and predicted its failure on the basis that its member states, which were underdeveloped and poor, would compete individually for markets and would give little attention to collective resolutions. Contrary to this perception, the organization continued to strengthen its administrative and technical structures and the activities of its headquarters continued to expand.

Second Stage: 1966–70

During this period the international oil companies started to show some interest in the activities of the organization and to open a dialogue with it. OPEC was able to extract from the oil companies certain concessions which the companies had considered to be their prerogative, such as reducing posted prices for marketing expenses, as well as the prices for long-term contracts. OPEC successfully convinced the oil companies that oil royalties should be counted as a portion of the general expenses of oil production to be subtracted from other costs from the general income prior to computing income tax. The oil companies used to consider such royalties as a portion of income tax, contrary to norms in the United States and other countries which considered royalties given to landowners as a portion of the general expenses subtracted from income prior to computing income tax on profits.

During this period, the foreign oil companies began to understand the position of the oil-producing countries which was logical and fair. In the past, the oil companies had implemented what was in their interest and what they considered in the interest of their countries, even at the expense of oil-producing countries. They used to give discounts on posted prices, in certain cases reaching 18 percent, and other discounts for so-called marketing expenses. They used to purchase oil from their operating companies, which produced oil for the parent companies, and would sell it to their refineries and/or affiliates. In other words, these discounts used to go to the pockets of the parent companies at the expense of the host countries.

Third Stage: 1971–75

This period of OPEC's history was the most fertile and productive, as the organization extricated itself from the stranglehold of the oil companies. OPEC was able to adjust oil prices upward more than four-fold in 1973 and 1974. At the end of 1973 prices were adjusted upward to US $5.15/bbl. and again in 1974 to US $11.80/bbl. Throughout the 1960s, the oil companies impeded any increase in oil prices at a time when prices of imports by OPEC countries from oil-consuming countries were increasing. The pressure exerted by the oil companies led to an explosive situation. OPEC countries had tried to negotiate with the oil companies to increase oil prices to a level more in line with the cost of generating energy from alternative sources (for example, the cost of oil from shale rocks or coal then ranged between US $17 and US $21/bbl.). The oil companies offered to increase the price of heavy oil from the Arabian Gulf by only six cents per barrel. It became obvious that the positions of the two parties were beyond reconciliation.

In 1969 the Libyan Revolution brought the monarchy to an end and young Libyan military officers came into power. The revolutionary government was convinced that the previous regime was under the stranglehold of the foreign oil companies. That regime permitted the oil companies to increase production to 3,600,000 barrels per day. The oil companies operating in Libya undermined the government by giving themselves large discounts on posted prices of oil. The government's take from oil was meager compared to the profits accrued to the oil companies from their different operations. However, the large oil production of Libya and the few projects implemented by the previous regime, left the country with large financial surpluses that strenghtened the negotiating stand of the new regime which now demanded that the terms of concessions and the programming of oil production be improved. The revolutionary government also demanded that posted oil prices be raised to a level that took into account the high quality of

Libyan oil, which is almost sulphur free, and the good geographic location of Libya in terms of transport cost. When the oil companies began to drag their feet in meeting these demands, the revolutionary government took unilateral action to implement them. It began negotiations with Occidental Oil Company, a small company operating in California and Canada. Occidental was able, through devious means, to obtain a concession from the monarchical regime in areas relinquished by some major oil companies, particularly Exxon. The latter had made big oil discoveries near the relinquished areas where Occidental was able to land a concession. Occidental was successful in making big discoveries in its concession and invested large sums of money in Europe in marketing the Libyan crude oil. The Libyan revolutionary government asked Occidental to improve the terms of its oil concession and to draw plans for the conservation of its oil production. Because of the financial reserves left over from the monarchical regime, the revolutionary government showed no interest in making more money and asked the oil companies to reduce oil production and increase prices. It also warned them that it would close the oil fields and stop oil exports if they did not meet its demands. The oil companies offered to increase the oil prices in line with their offer in the Gulf, but the Libyan government demanded that oil prices be increased by at least US $1.00 a barrel. All the oil companies, with the exception of Occidental, refused to meet the demands of the Libyan government. Occidental had no alternative but to accept those demands because it could not stop its oil production. It needed to supply its refineries and marketing facilities in Europe, and it was committed to oil sales agreements. The government then asked the rest of the oil companies to accede to the new terms or halve oil production. The oil companies had no alternative but to tow the same line.

The achievement of the Libyan revolutionary government was a turning point in the history of OPEC. It taught other members of OPEC that each one of them was ultimately responsible for its economic and political interests. After much frustration in attempting to convince the oil companies to accept their point of view, they adopted the Libyan method to bring them around. In 1973 and 1974 OPEC became a real force and oil prices were adjusted upward more than fourfold. The posted price of marker oil, which was exported from Ras Tanura, Saudi Arabia, with an API 34° degree and a sulphur content of 1.7 percent, became US $11.80 per barrel.

Financial Oil Surpluses and Their Negative Impacts on OPEC States

It became clear to OPEC, after its membership included most of the important oil producers and exporters, that it could achieve the aspirations of its people as long as it remained unified in dealing with the oil companies affiliated with the large industrialized states. OPEC's united stand enabled the organization to adjust upward the posted prices of oil more than fourfold.

When oil prices were adjusted upward in October 1973 and once more in January 1974, oil income accruing to these countries increased many-fold. However, most OPEC states were poor and developing countries with no other sources of income aside from oil. Even when some of these countries had some natural resources, they were unable to develop them and lacked the needed plans prior to the upward adjustment of oil prices. Therefore the windfall income from oil was not channeled properly. Oil countries with money reserves lacked the proper investment climate and found their reserves slipping back to banks and other financial institutions of the oil-consuming countries (particularly the United States and Western Europe), thereby diluting the benefits of the fourfold adjustment in oil prices. The fact that some OPEC member states were able to accumulate large financial surpluses in their balance of payments means that they were producing large quantities of oil in excess of what was needed to develop their economies. This situation would not serve the national interest of these countries in the long run.

The negative effects of the financial surpluses manifested themselves in various ways. This is because surplus fund countries dramatically increased their imports of consumer goods from industrialized countries. Further, prices of imported capital goods have increased three- to fourfold since 1972. In other words, the industrialized countries have not been passive toward the OPEC pricing decision. When OPEC countries adjusted oil prices, which had remained frozen for ten years by the oil companies, the industrialized countries reacted by raising fourfold the price of capital goods. This situation adversely affected the development plans of OPEC countries and raised questions regarding the viability of their development programs due to the high cost of capital goods and services. The decline of the surpluses of OPEC countries after 1975 resulted from the depreciating value of the dollar, inflation, and the high cost of development due to the increased cost of import goods and services from industrialized countries. This situation forced OPEC countries to increase their production to meet the higher cost of economic development plans.

The purchasing power of the dollar took a nose dive in recent years. This has adversely affected oil-producing states. The erosion of the purchasing power of the dollar—the currency used for oil payments—inflation, and the fourfold increase in the price of capital goods and services have resulted in a decrease of money surpluses since 1974 and adversely affected the economies of OPEC states, particularly those which did not realize money surpluses.

As the oil demand decreases annually, the purchasing power of the dollar drops in real terms and inflationary forces in the industrialized countries continue unabated. The combined impact cannot but be harmful to oil-producing countries. It is estimated that these countries lost 22.5 percent of the value of their oil exports between 1974 and 1978. According to these estimates, losses for 1976, 1977, and 1978 amount to approximately US $53 billion. Since oil prices were adjusted upward in 1974 and until 1978, OPEC countries received US $550 billion, of which US $400 billion were spent in oil-consuming countries for goods, services, and arms.

Development Plans in OPEC Countries: An Assessment

The upward adjustment of oil prices in 1973–74 and again in 1979–80, presented OPEC members with the opportunity to draw development plans for improving the life of their people, ensuring the continuity of this life, and ultimately diversifying their economies away from oil, a depletable asset. The first thrust was to process the oil in their own countries, particularly to increase their refining capacity. With the exception of Venezuela, these countries refine only 5 percent of their oil exports—a small percentage by any standards.

When these countries opened negotiations with manufacturers in industrialized states to build new refining facilities or expand existing ones, they discovered that the cost of new refineries had multiplied. Added to this, the oil companies and the industrialized countries discouraged attempts by OPEC countries to build new refineries, so that petroleum products from these refineries would not compete with their own. When some oil producers resisted such pressures and went ahead with their plans to build industries based on oil, the industrialized countries found this to be a golden opportunity to extract their payments for oil in the easiest manner. Development plans in the Arabian Gulf and North Africa went ahead, but at a cost unheard of in the oil industry. Cost of refineries, petrochemical plants, hydroelectric plants, have all escalated to billions of dollars instead of hundreds of millions for the largest units. OPEC countries faced repercussions in their drive to build these plants, the most important of which are:

- Between 2.5 and 3 million skilled and unskilled alien workers converged on OPEC countries. Their annual wages are estimated around US $5.5 billion.
- It is estimated that the cost of building a refinery in the Arabian Gulf is 2.5 to 3 times that of a similar size refinery in the Gulf of Mexico or Western Europe.
- The markets to which oil products from OPEC countries could be exported are saturated with manufacturing plants. Further, the cost plant construction and operation in the Gulf area (which in the long term needs expatriate manpower) makes it impossible for these goods to compete successfully with those manufactured in the United States, Europe, or Japan. If these development plans are allowed to continue without adjusting their nature and objectives, they will prove to be a burden on the oil industry rather than a boost. Oil exporters will eventually find out that the industrialized countries have done them more harm through raising the cost of building and servicing these plants than the harm—if any—that OPEC caused them as a result of adjusting oil prices upward. This adjustment, in fact, made it possible to develop oil in the North slope of Alaska and the North Sea.
- Oil exporters have no alternative but to try to reach an agreement with the industrialized countries regarding their plans for development. Oil producers and consumers could cooperate in sharing the cost of exploration for oil and increasing reserves, in building refineries, petrochemical plants and tankers, and in liquification and transport of gas.

If the above avenue of cooperation is not possible, oil producers should think of their interest, the future of their people, and the preservation of their rights by gradually reducing oil production to about half its present level and investing in other sources of energy. Further, oil producers should employ part of their money, which is invested abroad, in developing agricultural projects in their states. Developing agriculture is a pressing matter for the oil-producing countries, as most of them import agricultural products. In case of crisis between the oil producers and consumers, oil consumers who are agricultural producers, such as the United States and some European countries, could use the food weapon if OPEC countries used the oil weapon. Some of the oil countries have large agricultural potentialities. Agricultural development is a process which can run in perpetuity and, in the long run, it is less costly than investing in petrochemicals which are controlled by the industrialized countries.

Arab–Latin American Cooperation

Cooperation between the Arab oil producers and Venezuela was instrumental in the formation of OPEC in 1960. Their joint efforts within OPEC led to the increase of oil prices in 1973-74 to a fair and just level. In light of the industrialized countries' continuous efforts to depress the price of oil through inflation and decrease the benefits of the oil producers by unreasonably increasing the cost of their development programs, it is imperative that cooperation between Arab and Latin American members of OPEC continue. In a broader sense, cooperation should be extended to other Arab and Latin American countries on a regional basis. The following considerations must be kept in mind:

* In their attempt to reduce their dependence on industrialized countries, oil producers in particular must develop better economic relations with other developing countries. This would enable them to create a more balanced exchange of resources and technology among themselves and reduce the bargaining power of industrialized countries.
* More advanced Latin American countries, such as Brazil, Argentina, and Mexico can help Arab countries in their industrialization programs and provide management training in various production and service sectors.
* The need of Arab oil producers to develop their petrochemical industry and the need of Latin American countries for oil could be satisfied by mutual cooperation. Advanced Latin American countries could help Arab oil producers in oil refining and petrochemical diversification in exchange for secured oil supply.

The Arab and Latin American peoples have many things in common and this will make it easy for them to appreciate their development problems and cooperate in their solution. The cooperation of Arab and Latin American oil producers proved to be beneficial in the past. The well-being of their people hinges upon their further cooperation.

4

The Need for More Horizontal Cooperation on Oil between Latin American and Arab Countries

Amaury Porto de Oliveira

To speak of relations between Latin America and the Arab world in the energy fields is to speak of oil and OPEC. All of us are aware of the decision contributions of Pablo Pérez Alfonso, a Venezuelan, and of Abdullah Tariki, a Saudi Arabian, to the birth of the Organization of Petroleum Exporting Countries (OPEC). Now a second Latin American country, Ecuador, is a member of that predominantly Arab organization. OPEC archives will one day provide historians with evidence of the decision role Latin American-Arab cooperation played in the development of OPEC. There were, for example, the discussions between Venezuela and Libya in 1969 as a result of violations by foreign concession holders of oil-field conservation standards. The resulting measures imposed by Tripoli to protect its national wealth were crucial to the sudden emergence of OPEC in 1973 as a major force on the international scene. Abdullah Tariki himself, drawing on his tremendous expertise, has given us an account of the history of OPEC and its worldwide impact. Let us turn our attention to the future and one little-studied facet of the larger energy problem that offers unlimited possibilities for Latin American-Arab cooperation: how to meet the oil needs of oil-importing countries of the Third World.

Much has been written in the last ten years about the energy future of mankind. But, as Jean-Romain Frisch recently pointed out, in all this mass of writings the needs of the Third World are usually treated as a factor to be rounded off in projections dealing mainly with the problems of industrialized nations. "Nearly always dealt with as a single entity and without regard to regional differences, the Third World is rarely examined from non-traditional standpoints to obtain conclusions that are not mere extrapolations of trends."[1] A thorough and carefully designed study of Third World energy prospects was submitted to the XI world Energy Conference (Munich, September 1980) by the Committee on Energy Problems of Developing Countries, set up at the X Conference (Istanbul, September 1977). From the text of this study, available to the general public,[2] we have excerpted a few statements that help focus our theme:

- In the absence of a prolonged economic recession or grave political crisis that would seriously block its chances for development, the Third World's share of world energy consumption will probably grow from 25 percent in 1976 to 40 percent by the year 2000, and to 50 percent by 2020.
- As a consequence of the population explosion, Third World per capita energy consumption will remain low: in the year 2020 one out of two persons will still consume at the level currently regarded as the development threshold (0.8 ton petroleum equivalent [tpe] per capital).
- Two regions of the Third World—Latin America and the Middle East —will probably have improved the well-being of their population. By the year 2020 average energy consumption in those two regions could reach 2.5 tpe per capita, slightly below the average level of Western Europe in the 1960s.

The predictions of the same study regarding the composition of the Third World energy balance in the year 2020 are interesting:

- Traditional noncommercial energy sources: a predictable drop in consumption to not more than 7-16 percent of total consumption.
- Hydroelectric energy: may increase to 3,100-3,500 trillion watt hours (TWH)—twice the current world production.
- New energy sources: 23 percent of total consumption.
- Coal: 3 percent of total consumption. Coal is likely to be a significant source only in Asian countries with a centrally planned economy (principally China) and in Latin American countries such as Brazil or Colombia.
- Nuclear energy: may reach 9 percent of the total, depending on the outcome of uncertainties surrounding its development.
- Natural gas: will probably continue to increase, reaching 11 percent of total consumption.
- Oil: the energy source that, owing to its inherent qualities, best meets the needs of countries that began economic modernization after the coal age had passed. The Third World will have more difficulty in overcoming oil dependency than the industrialized countries. Third World oil consumption alone could surpass current world production

by the year 2010. By 2020 oil could represent 32 percent of all energy consumed by Third World nations.

This brief overview leads us to two conclusions: First, the special medium-term responsibility of the countries of Latin America, the Middle East (in particular Arab countries), and the Third World generally for their own energy future, and second, the growing importance of oil to these nations, despite the sizable contribution other energy sources may make to their energy balance. In addition, there are tremendous opportunities for Arab–Latin American cooperation on issues other than oil. It remains to be seen how and to what extent oil can serve as the basis for cooperation between Arab and Latin American countries. Their OPEC members have already done a great deal to assist their Third World counterparts in overcoming problems created by higher oil prices. However, OPEC has its own battles to fight with the industrialized world. The issue is to define an arena in which developing countries, OPEC members or not, can cooperate in the solution of specific problems.

At present (mid-1981) the international oil system is faced with two major questions: Has world oil demand began its historic decline? Has the price of a barrel of crude oil reached a level at which it is economically advantageous for the industrialized world to invest in replacement energy sources? On all sides we see evidence of a strong and continuing drop in oil consumption by industrialized countries. There are indications that OPEC is concerned about the possibility that these nations may already be in a position to develop alternatives to oil before exporting countries can free themselves from their dependence on the oil industry as their sole source of survival.

Exxon gave a warning signal in December 1980. In its customary end-of-the-year forecast of energy developments, Exxon indicated that world energy consumption in the year 2000 would be about 225 million barrels per day (b/d) of oil or oil equivalents, including 70 million b/d of conventional oil and 7 million b/d of synthetic oil. Seeing that in 1979 total world oil consumption was 66 million b/d, Exxon's prediction of 77 million b/d for all types of oil by the year 2000 represents a significant drop in the growth rate for oil demand. In its 1979 end-of-the-year forecast, using an $18 a barrel price for crude oil, the company predicted a 1 percent annual growth rate in oil demand through the end of the century. By the end of 1980, using data for the period May-October, when the average price of a barrel of crude oil had already reached $32, Exxon cut its predicted annual growth rate for oil demand to 0.5 percent.[3]

Now, six months later, even this reduced estimate by Exxon in its predicted growth rate of demand is regarded as excessive. The explanation lies partly with the economic recession in industrialized countries and partly with the growing use of coal, natural gas, and nuclear energy as replacement fuels for some oil uses. In the main, it is the result of increased energy conservation with both reduced consumption (changes in the way people use their motor vehicles, lower lighting and heating levels) and more efficient energy use (improved industrial production methods, smaller and lighter cars, better insulation of buildings). World demand for oil has fallen in a way that dims even the most pessimistic predictions. The weekly magazine *The Economist* gave this description of the situation in Great Britain:

> Britain is driving away from oil at a speed that is alarming the oil companies. Total oil consumption dropped about 16 percent last year to 1.4m barrels a day (over 70m metric tonnes a year), its lowest for 15 years, and is likely to fall 8 percent this year (1981).
>
> It is the steepest decline in oil consumption of all the industrialized countries. . . . British oil marketing men who in the early 1970's dreamed of Britain oil demand reaching 2.8 barrels a day (twice last year's level) are now talking of a "historical turning point."[4]

Meanwhile, in the United States the major oil companies are lamenting the big drop in their first quarter earnings for 1981. The windfall profits tax left the companies with only 15 to 20 percent of the increase in prices resulting from decontrol of domestic oil. Even more disturbing, with a sharp drop in demand for petroleum products, they will be unable to pass on to the consumer the increase in costs since the beginning of the year. Gasoline and heating oil are going unwanted despite the fact that refineries are operating at only 68.75 percent of capacity.[5]

As for the risk of reaching the point where OPEC is no longer able to market its oil, the Saudi oil minister himself has indicated that possibility. In a lecture he delivered in January 1981 to students at the University of Petroleum and Mines in Dammam, Sheik Ahmed Zaki Yamani stated: "If we force Western countries to invest heavily in finding alternate sources of energy, they will. This would take no more than seven or ten years and would result in reducing dependence on oil as a source of energy to a point which will jeopardize Saudi Arabia's interests. . . . This picture is based on scientific studies, and is supported by facts and figures available to OPEC and to agencies of our Ministry of Petroleum."[6] According to Sheik Yamani, studies by impartial analysts show OPEC's share of the world oil market may fall in the near future to 22 million b/d. Exxon's predictions of December 1980 were more optimistic: 30 million b/d in 1990 and 29 million b/d in the year 2000.

It is not our purpose to seek a definitive answer to doubts surrounding the future of oil. The issues go to the heart of the relationship between OPEC and the industrialized member countries of the OCED, a relationship in which economic factors frequently take second place to political considerations fully understood only by those directly involved. My concern as a citizen of a developing, oil-importing nation is the impact of the future oil situation on countries like my own: How to guarantee such countries an adequate supply of oil. From the standpoint of oil-importing developing or underdeveloped countries, the increasing trend toward reduced world oil production is damaging from any point of view.

Historically the tendency of industrialized countries to seek greater energy efficiency through technological progress seems inevitable. The International Institute for Applied Systems Analysis (Laxenburg, Austria) has been studying this trend, noticeable since the beginning of the Industrial Revolution, toward ever more efficient use of energy. Greater efficiency is achieved by more economical use of the current energy source and/or by using forms of energy that are successively more versatile, i.e., capable of producing economic benefits greater than the cost of installing the worldwide infrastructure necessary for its use. On the basis of this traditional strategy of minimizing costs, the industrialized countries have not only limited their oil consumption, but are also attempting to replace oil with more profitable forms of energy such as uranium, hydrogen, and, ideally, solar energy.[7]

It also seems inevitable and just that OPEC countries should reject the manner in which industrialized countries treat OPEC oil production when forecasting world oil supplies. Traditionally industrialized countries take the established estimate for world oil demand, subtract the amount corresponding to centrally planned economies, calculate the portion that will be covered by their own production and that of non-OPEC developing nations, and proclaim the remainder as OPEC's share of the market. The actual or potential reduction of OPEC's share is even viewed with satisfaction as the road to the "destruction of OPEC." One of the principal manifestations of the new state of affairs in the international oil system has been the ability and determination of OPEC countries to first calculate the production level most consonant with their own national interests and then offer to the market whatever remains after supplying their own domestic demand.

However just and inevitable the above processes, they are likely to reduce—even in absolute terms—the amount of oil available to the rest of the world through the end of the century. From the point of view of the developing and underdeveloped countries, this is a violation of the global obligation that the international oil system seemed to have assumed. Latin Americans in general and Brazilians in particular are not surprised. Experience has taught Latin Americans that there are two oil worlds. There is the international system composed of the industrial-commercial complex built by the multinational oil companies of the OCED area supported by the production and export of crude oil from the former concession areas. Then there is the world of national experiences in which locally produced oil is principally a factor of internal development.

The countries of the former concession areas joined forces in OPEC and waged a brilliant campaign to assert the interests of member countries against those of the multinationals. However, the main thrust of OPEC's political and economic policies, as its own documents openly state, is based on the logic of the industrialized economies. The second oil world is composed of countries (nearly all of them developing or underdeveloped) that, because of an internal policy decision or because their oil resources did not attract the interest of the multinationals, remained outside the international oil system. The communist countries as a group constitute a special case that this chapter does not propose to examine.

We cannot recount here the entire history of the international oil system. This chapter will merely describe how, between 1928 and 1934, the principal multinational oil companies (the so-called Seven Sisters) entered into a series of agreements (the Achnacarry Agreement and others)[8] designed to structure the entire production and marketing system for petroleum derivatives, meaning the products refined from crude oil. We shall also briefly examine the way in which international oil production came to depend on a network of giant fields, defined as those capable of producing, during their useful life, a minimum of 500 million barrels of oil (a supergiant field can produce at least 5 billion barrels).

The critical event in the move to giant fields was the blowout in the United States (1930) of the East Texas field, the only supergiant field discovered to date in the continental United States (excluding Alaska). Prior to 1930 there were some giant fields already producing in the United States, and in their initial incursions into the world at large the major oil companies had already exhausted Mexico's Alameda de Oro field and had gone on to depend primarily on the supergiant Bolívar Costeiro field discovered in Venezuela in 1917.

East Texas, in addition to being extraordinarily large for a U.S. field, appeared outside the production and marketing framework set up by the big oil companies. It was discovered by a wildcatter and by the time the big companies realized what had happened, it had already been split up into thousands of lots that were snapped up by small owners. The appearance of wildcat oil in East Texas, together with the harsh economic depression of the early 1930s, brought down the price structure and division of international markets specified in the agreements among oil companies. The discovery of the East Texas field demonstrated that the degree of control already exercised by the international oil industry was not sufficient to ensure peaceful operation of the cartel.

The big oil companies reacted in several ways. In the United States the Connally Act (Hot Oil Act) of 1934 and the Field Conservation Acts (enforced against small producers at "gunpoint") established the necessary conditions for future control of any outbreaks of wildcat oil. In the concession areas they managed to react to the sudden glut of oil by cutting back on local production (in Iraq and Venezuela, for example). The companies organized themselves so as to digest the giant and supergiant fields around the world.[9] In short, an important factor came into play. In the words of Thierry de Monbrial: "The oil industry is characterized by its need for oganization. In periods of growing profits competition alone is unable to exercise long-term control over behavior, since this would lead to continuing reclassification of the fields and, as a result, the elimination of some producers as new discoveries were made. One possible response is to organize the industry in such a way as to minimize the effects of chance. . . . This is the larger framework that makes the history of the oil industry understandable from its inception to the end of the 1960s."[10]

Richard Nehring, the well-known Rand Corporation analyst, did an extensive study in 1978 of the role of the giant and supergiant fields as the backbone of the international oil system. He listed 272 fields with a production potential of over 500 million barrels, discovered in 1859-1975, that by 1975 had supplied 76.7 percent of the world's production and proven reserves. The remaining 23.3 percent were furnished by 30,000 small and medium-size fields.[11] Thirty-three of the 272 fields listed by Nehring fall into the category of supergiants and accounted for over half the production and proven reserves through 1975. The author stresses the importance of these fields: "The growth in known recoverable oil resources and in annual world production during the past half-century has resulted primarily from the discovery and development of super-giant oil fields. These fields provided the bulk of the easy and extremely inexpensive additions to reserves and production capacity that produced the real decline in world oil prices in the 25 years before 1973. They account for the pre-eminence of the Middle East among all the producing regions of the world.''[12] It was not until 1950 that Middle Eastern oil production surpassed that of Latin America. During 1918-49 Latin America was second in production only to the United States. Venezuela, 99 percent of whose production was controlled by three of the Seven Sisters (Exxon, Shell, and Gulf), supplied 40 percent of the international oil trade.

A reexamination of the history of this trade, using the two–oil world thesis, contradicts the oft-repeated explanation that Latin American nationalism drove the big oil companies from the region. It furnishes evidence that these same companies had only a limited and fragmented interest in Latin America. Beginning in the nineteenth century some oil prospecting was done in every part of Latin America. While these efforts were mostly conducted by governments and national groups, it is also true that in the first three decades of this century the major American oil companies and Shell made a thorough survey of the region to ascertain its oil potential. This is described in detail in the monumental history of the worldwide search for oil published by the American Association of Petroleum Geologists.[13] What the companies learned in this initial assessment clearly influenced their future behavior toward Latin America. In the world of fifty years ago only Mexico and Venezuela had sufficient productive capacity to attract the international system then being established. Mexico rejected the system (nationalization in 1938), but Venezuela was tightly bound to it. By 1938, five giant fields (including the supergiant Bolívar Costeiro) had already been discovered in Venezuela, a country that in Nehring's most recent list was represented by thirteen of the twenty-seven giant fields located in Latin America. Also in 1938 the process of "unification of Venezuelan production," fully described in a famous report by the U.S. Federal Trade Commission, was completed. This consisted of extending to Venezuela the series of intercompany agreements beginning with the Achnacarry Agreement.[14]

The handful of other Latin American countries in which big oil maintained some interest all have giant fields: Peru (one), Colombia (one), the Trinidad and Tobago (two). The sudden interest in Ecuador at the end of the 1960s stemmed from the discovery there of two giant fields. And if the multinationals never completely abandoned Argentina, even during the heyday of Yacimientos Petrolíferos Fiscales, it was perhaps with an eye to the future. The southern coast of Argentina and Mexico's Bay of Campeche are considered the two Latin American areas with undeveloped oil potential capable of affecting the world oil supply.

It would be useless to reopen the debate that gripped two generations of Latin Americans—the question of whether less economic nationalism would have permitted Latin America to reap more benefit from its oil resources. The lesson of history is that we deceive ourselves if we imagine that the international system would have optimized the development of oil resources everywhere. Its focus, beginning in the 1930s, on giant fields was motivated by two powerful factors. The first was the Field Conservation Acts. These introduced the so-called market allotments into the United States and raised the marginal cost of production of a barrel of Texas oil to a level that determined the international price of a barrel of crude oil,[15] and thus ensured that any producer who controlled the extremely low unit cost production made possible by the giant fields stood to reap fabulous returns on capital. The second factor was that these giant fields enjoyed the further and all-important advantage of "excess productive capacity," the option of easily raising or lowering local production in response to market demand.

Going back to our description of the international oil system as an industrial-commercial complex built by the multinational oil companies on the basis of crude oil from the concession areas (today the OPEC member nations), it is undeniably true that the system always behaved in response to the needs of the industrialized economies. Before OPEC took up the fight there were no national development experiences based on oil within the concession areas. The international system was exclusively concerned with ensuring a supply and demand balance for oil in the world based on calculations of the relative scarcity or surplus of petroleum products in the industrialized world. Never did their calculations take into account the growing energy needs of developing countries.

Even production areas integrated into the international system, for example Iraq, were developed solely in accordance with the international commercial strategy. Iraq is one of the world's most oil-rich countries. Yet the Iraq Petroleum Company, composed of BP, Shell, Exxon, Mobil, and the Compagnie Française des Pétroles, which together with two local subsidiaries held the concession for all the Iraqi territory, only developed about 0.5 percent of that country's productive capacity. It is public knowledge that for a variety of reasons the Seven Sisters gave priority to developing the oil resources of Iran and Saudi Arabia and held Iraqi production to a level below the other two.[16]

Up until the beginning of the energy crisis in the early 1970s there was a conspiracy of silence in the industrialized world on the subject of oil as a raw material. The vertically integrated system established by the big oil companies facilitated a kind of sleight of hand that kept oil out of the public eye. What the public saw was the magical appearance of oil products at one end of the system while hearing stories of dollars flowing into the distant coffers of Arab sheiks. Oil was absent even from UN debates and publications on raw materials. At the very most it rated an occasional footnote. The explanation given for the separate treatment accorded this natural resource was that oil figures would distort the general picture of raw material activities. So successfully had the multi-nationals segregated oil from the natural economic evolution of the concession areas, that this claim was largely true.

Inevitably, the ability of the industrialized world to stand on a base of natural resources located in underdeveloped countries encountered structural limitations. Professor Nurul Islam, in a recent article, points to a neglected facet of the overall oil question when he refers to the reversal of positions that occurred with energy minerals relative to the traditional behavior of industrialized countries. History demonstrates that over the years the distribution of mineral production remained relatively stable, one-half remaining with the development countries and the other half more or less equally divided between the undeveloped countries and those with centrally planned economies. In the case of oil, however, a change occurred in this classic pattern between 1950 and 1970. The share of the nonindustrialized countries grew from 17 to 40 percent, while that of the developed countries fell from 65 to 32 percent.[17]

This change resulted from the race by the big oil companies to the giant and supergiant fields of the concession areas. The same phenomenon produced the sudden strenghtening of the oil-exporting countries, which joined together in OPEC. The big oil companies beat a swift retreat back to the industrialized world (development of the North Sea and Arctic slope oil, large-scale resumption of U.S. offshore oil drilling, etc.) in a movement that is still going strong, further evidence that the multinationals were incapable of fully developing oil production everywhere.

The two major imponderables that weigh on the medium-term future of the international oil system have arisen from within the industrialized world. The key factor in the changes of perspective taking place in the international oil business lies in a setback suffered by the big oil companies at the hands of OPEC, namely the sudden loss by the Seven Sisters at the end of 1978, of the supply of "surplus" crude they had held until that point.

For decades the major oil companies dominated the international oil system through total control of the world supply and flow of crude oil. Beginning in 1972 OPEC launched a systematic attack on that control by increasing the host governments' share of the stock in the companies holding concessions in each of the member countries. The host country's share rose rapidly from 25 percent in 1972 to 51, 60, and even 100 percent in some cases. However, even when the host governments gained full ownership control, they continued to permit the former concession holders to market abroad a considerable portion of the oil produced. As late as mid-1978 this allowed the Seven Sisters to meet the needs of all their subsidiaries around the world while maintaining a surplus of about 3.7 million b/d. In the hands of the oil companies this "excess" crude was a powerful instrument with which to continue to exercise control over the international oil system.

In December 1978 the total cutoff of Iranian oil exports meant a loss to the Seven Sisters of 3.3 million b/d, depriving them of their valuable surplus, which they never recovered. The chain reactions set off by this fact produced the chaos that reigned throughout 1979 in the Rotterdam spot market (in May 1980 the spot market price for a barrel of Arabian light was already $20 above Saudi Arabia's official price of $12.70) and continued to be felt in all the successive changes in the international oil system.[18] The bargaining power of OPEC member countries increased tremendously, which enabled them to largely free themselves from their dependence on the big oil companies for marketing their production abroad. They began to market more of their crude directly and renegotiated their contracts with the former concession holders on much more favorable terms. Suddenly the oil companies began to feel that oil was not such a good deal after all.

Underlying much of what began to be published about the "beginning of the historic decline in oil demand" were purely strategic business considerations. At the annual meeting of British Petroleum in London on April 2, 1981, BP chairman Sir David Steel was very explicit: "When one looks ahead, oil and gas no longer appear to be a great industry." Steel then predicted what BP was likely to look like in another decade. Oil and gas would represent no more than 50 percent of the company's investments. Between 10 and 12 percent would be invested in the chemical industry, another 8 percent in coal, and the rest in sectors such as nutrition and detergents. Such diversification, Steel stressed, would not result simply from a desire to spend money, but from a need to ensure a renewed cash flow for the company.[19]

Public statements such as that of BP's chairman of the broad's, together with all the sensational news of big oil company acquisitions of nonoil companies and even non–energy related companies, creates the impression that the multinationals are gearing up for the postoil era. OPEC nations, in turn, in a legitimate effort to safeguard their economies and prolong the useful life of their principal nonrenewable resource, are progressively limiting their oil production, which in any case will be increasingly consumed at home. The result is that world oil production is being sharply cut back. While this may be in the interest of the two blocks that make up the system, it darkens the prospects for oil-importing countries of the developing and underdeveloped world. The abundant supply of cheap oil the international system created for its own purposes in the past induced these countries to make virtually the whole of their economic modernization programs oil dependent.

The time has come to speak of the other oil world, the world of countries which, whether or not possess oil wealth, need, now more than ever, to resolve the problem of their oil supply on their own national terms. For countries that have already gone a part of the way, like Mexico and Brazil, as well as for countries that have barely begun, oil has become a vital commodity. In the 1920s and 1930s Brazilian oil prospects were also surveyed by the major oil companies, but failed to spark their interest.[20] Only in 1940, when Brazil itself had already begun to develop the Reconcayo basin in Bahia and had established the National Oil Council (CNP), did one of the Seven Sisters (specifically Exxon) propose, without much enthusiasm, to "cooperate with the Government in the solution of the oil problem" in Brazil.[21] The proposal did not suit the Brazilians, who were about to launch one of the most successful experiments in dealing with the oil question on their own national terms.

Until the mid-1970s all drilling and oil production in Brazil was done by the CNP and, from 1953 on, by Brazilian Petroleum Inc. (Petrobras). CNP turned over to Petrobras rigs and fields capable of producing 2,700 b/d of crude oil along with a refinery with a 5,000 b/d capacity, at a time when total national oil consumption had already reached 160,000 b/d. Unfortunately Brazilian geology has not yet lived up to the dream of oil abundance that has always captured the Brazilian imagination. For all its efforts both on land and offshore, Petrobras has yet to raise Brazilian production above a quarter of a million barrels per day.[22] Yet Petrobras has been one of the mainstays of Brazil's extraordinary economic expansion of the last twenty years. Having chosen an economic model based on a motor-vehicle industry (one million cars, buses, trucks, and tractors produced each year), Brazil began to consume over a million barrels of oil a day. Year after year, thanks to its work overseas, including prospecting and producing in other countries, and thanks even more to its international bargaining power, Petrobras has always managed to ensure an adequate supply of oil for Brazil. By the mid-1960s, having acquired a modern network of refineries, Petrobras made Brazil self-sufficient in petroleum products.

The immense gap between Brazil's oil production and consumption demonstrates how absurd it would be to extend to the Third World the same concept of surplus and scarcity that prevails in the operation of the international oil system. Such surpluses and scarcities are always relative to the ups and downs of market cycles. Even today, the attempt to definitively cap demand has very little to do with actual oil reserves, which are still quite abundant. The "end" of oil reflects more than anything else the irreversible move of industrialized societies to more versatile forms of energy use, and the capital-formation strategy of the big oil companies. However, the problem facing Third World countries, now and for a long time into the future, is how to increase their use of oil.

An awareness of this problem—the imperative need to promptly ensure an oil supply for the Third World—has begun to concern international agencies. OPEC has addressed the need through a number of encouraging proposals included in its long-range strategy. Regional agencies like the Latin American Energy Organization (OLADE) and the Organization of Arab Petroleum Exporting Countries (OAPEC) have kept the issue on their agendas. Beginning in 1979, the World Bank began a loan program to finance Third World energy projects. The Inter-American Development Bank has also made loans for this purpose. Recently (The Hague, March 16-20, 1981) the United Nations organized a conference on strategies for oil development in developing countries. The scope of this chapter does not permit a review of everything that has been said or done in these various forums, much less an evaluation of the ideas discussed or the initiatives approved. I shall simply attempt to define, amid the great body of existing opinions and conclusions, where the interest of countries such as my own lies, starting from the premise of the existence of two oil worlds.

Let us first delineate the area on which we wish to focus. In the second oil world, oil use is not a function of the market in which one turns to oil when it is readily available at low prices and to "conservation" and alternative sources when prices are high. In these countries "energy saving" is not an option. On the contrary, they require large injections of energy. Aside from possible hydroelectric resources (of which Brazil, for example, has made extensive use) and innovative programs such as Brazil's use of alcohol for motor fuel, oil use is inevitable. In the countries under discussion, very little of their economic development has depended on coal or railroads. Modernization has been based almost entirely on oil, as is shown by the well-documented fact that, since World War II, Third World oil consumption has grown 50 percent faster than its increase in total energy consumption.

Current estimates of the world's oil resources seem unacceptable.

Peter R. Odell, one of the experts most active in analyzing the many facets of the energy issue, rigorously examined the statement that the planet's ultimate oil reserves (the sum of oil already extracted from the subsoil and that which still remains) are approximately two trillion (2^{10}) barrels. Working together with K.E. Rosing and researchers of the Erasmus University of Rotterdam's Economisch Geografisch Institut,[23] he showed how the aforementioned statement became accepted as a dogma during the 1970s as a result of the "energy crisis." However, two trillion barrels of oil is an extremely pessimistic estimate. Soviet estimates, for example, which may err in the other direction, are in the order of eleven trillion barrels. Until the beginning of the 1970s the multinationals themselves were calmly optimistic about the abundance of available oil "for many years to come." The Rotterdam professors cite a discussion in which R.A. Sickler, of Shell Oil's Exploration and Production Division, admitted that, in insisting on the figure of two trillion barrels, the major oil companies were not really seeking an accurate tally of the world's resources. The two trillion figure was simply a "logistically limited" estimate "conditioned by the existing climate [for exploration and development] and the prospects [for increasing the reserves] up to about the year 2000."[24] In other words, the world oil horizon is fixed by the commercial strategy of the major oil companies.

The multinationals have made their assessment of world oil resources, reducing or even discounting the potential of entire regions, conditional upon the vagaries of international politics and the militancy with which Third World countries defend their own economic interests. At the aforementioned UN meeting it was once again Peter Odell who pointed out that the big oil companies neglected to update their figures for certain areas of the Third World in light of new theories on the location of oil and gas deposits and rapidly evolving geological information. This is particularly striking in the case of Latin America, where the figures used by the companies only a few years ago have already been virtually overtaken by the proven, probable, and possible reserves of Mexico alone. It will be up to the countries of the second oil world, using their own means and working cooperatively, to correct the unreliable data and interpretations put forth by the international system and conditioned by its own logic.

Virtually 90 percent of the human and financial resources devoted to the production and distribution of oil under the international system are controlled by the industrialized world. Basing themselves on this fact the major oil companies have propagated the idea that there is only one oil industry and that it is international by definition. The "internationality" consisted of the subservience to the industrialized nucleus of low-cost production areas in which the companies could accumulate the tremendous profits required to offset the high production costs of their own region. When OPEC caused the multinationals to lose their gold mines in the former concession areas, the companies began to probe the planet with their risk contracts in search of new rivers of gold. At present there are a number of tax havens emerging in Western Africa, as the April 16, 1981 edition of *Arab Oil and Gas* pointed out. (There are examples in that area of countries where foreign companies are earning seven to ten dollars for each barrel of crude oil produced.) There is not however, any international equality in the reinvestment of profits. Figures show that most of the big oil company investments are being applied to the United States and to "safe areas" such as the North Sea and the Arctic slopes, most recently in the mining and natural resource sectors. This long-standing situation is characterized by Peter Odell as the "geographically distorted allocation of the production factors in the oil industry." Bernard F. Grossling, internationally known American geophysicist working for the Inter-American Development Bank, has compiled some impressive figures on the number of wells drilled. Of the 3 million exploratory and production wells drilled during the entire history of the oil industry, 2.2 million were drilled in the United States, a country that possesses no more than 10 percent of the world's potential oil-producing areas. The number of wells drilled in Latin America, on the other hand, was only 100,000, and in Africa only about 50,000.[25]

Traditionally, international credit institutions have refused financial aid to Third World countries for oil exploration. The standard justification is that, wherever there are real prospects for producing oil in commercial quantities, it will always be possible to interest the multinationals, which have sufficient funds of their own to develop any new area. In the last three years the World Bank has begun to finance the kind of project that was previously turned down. Recipients of this aid point to two main problems with the way in which it is being extended. First, implicit in those projects approved is the assumption that they will be implemented by one of the multinationals (the financing serves as insurance for the company that handles the project). Second, rarely is financing approved for drilling in new areas. The World Bank gives preference to development and production projects for known oil reserves or for the preliminary phases of oil exploration.[26]

It is becoming urgently necessary to conduct a systematic and determined search for oil in countries whose marginal potential was the very reason for their neglect by the multinationals. The Brazilian experience has shown the usefulness of building a national oil industry on a basis of limited oil reserves. For the vast majority of Third World countries their domestic oil potential will be more than sufficient to ensure at the very least a development takeoff. The greater the geographic diversification of oil production, the better, since it will give developing and underdeveloped countries more hope of meeting their energy needs in the historically inevitable context of high prices for international oil and cutbacks in OPEC production.

Having thus delimited the scope of the concept of a second oil world, let us conclude with some thoughts on how best to ensure that the non–oil–exporting countries of the Third World also have an energy future. The world is moving ever faster toward a new energy age. The industrialized countries are at the controls, carefully restructuring their production systems and engineering technological leaps to ensure their own continued economic growth based on renewable energy flows. Oil-exporting countries of the developing world—whether or not they are OPEC members—are also restructuring their economies to apply their current abundance of capital and oil to the construction of more stable and diversified economies. For oil-exporting countries the crucial point is not to allow the pace at which the industrialized world is freeing itself from its excessive dependence on oil to acclerate too fast relative to their own efforts at diversification.

Developing countries that are oil importers now face a twofold challenge. They must follow the rest of the world into the new energy era or be indefinitely relegated to the limbo of civilization. At the same time they must overcome their current capital and energy deficits. The central thesis of this chapter is that the efforts required on both these fronts can only be successful in the context of the second oil world. Meeting this twofold challenge will require a great deal of creative imagination. To the extent that these countries learn to take advantage of their own local characteristics, there is no limit to the energy sources available to them. (The Brazilian program of motor-grade alcohol is a good example of this. More experiences of this nature and an exchange of ideas on the subject can only be advantageous.) Yet for a long time to come oil will be the most appropriate energy source for the gigantic task of economic modernization facing the Third World. Inasmuch as the members of the international oil system are already committed to move beyond oil as the dominant energy source, it is up to those countries that are still much in need of oil to coordinate their efforts to obtain and use it in the context of national or regional programs.

The issue is moving ahead with existing efforts at horizontal South-South cooperation and devising new initiatives in all energy sectors.[27] The emphasis must inevitably be on the search for oil and its production in developing countries that are oil importers today. Sufficient experts and technical resources are available to get the job done, particularly in Latin America and the Arab countries, two regions that bear a special responsibility for promoting energy development in the Third World.

The response to the question of how to finance such initiatives must include OPEC. This is not a repetition of the same oil tune that OPEC must supply cheap oil to its colleagues in the Third World or divide its profits with them. OPEC countries, in this view, are like all other developing countries that have had the luck of the energy draw at the end of this century. Their specific interest in ensuring that the pace at which the world moves beyond oil dependence remains moderate is consistent with the general interests of the Third World, and they can only benefit from a happy solution to the problem of an energy supply for oil-importing nations of the developing world.[28]

Notes

1. Jean-Romain Frisch, "Avenir énergétique de Tiers-Monde" (energy future of the Third World), *Revue de l'Energie* (May 1981):207.
2. *Horizons énergétiques du Tiers-Monde, 2000-2020* (Third World energy horizons, 2000-2020) (Paris: Editions Techniques et Economiques, April 1981).
3. Cf. *Petroleum Intelligence Weekly*, New York, December 22, 1980, p.l.
4. "Britain's Glut," *The Economist*, April 4, 1981, p.25.
5. "U.S. Oil Companies Expect Big Earnings Drop in 1st Quarter," *International Herald Tribune*, March 31, 1981.
6. Unofficial translation of a lecture by Sheik Ahmed Zaki Yamani entitled "Petroleum: A Look into the Future," published as a special supplement to the *Petroleum Intelligence Weekly*, March 9, 1981. The quoted portions are from p. 3. In April 1981 the Western press echoed the forecasts indicated here, which came out of a Euro-Arab conference in Rome. In an article in the *Wall Street Journal*, April 13, 1981, Youssef M. Ibrahim quotes the deputy secretary of OPEC, Fadhil Al-Chalabi: "Substantially higher prices in real terms in the future will no doubt accelerate the pace of transition [of the industrialized economies to alternate energy sources], and hence speedily reduce OPEC's share of total energy requirements."
7. An excellent presentation of the work of the IIAAS on energy is offered by Wolfgang Sassin in *Scientific American*, September 1980, pp. 106-17.
8. The agreement on the division of the international market for oil products, known as the "As Is Agreement," was signed on September 17, 1928, at the Scottish village of Achnacarry. The original signatories were Exxon, Shell, and BP. Several months later Mobil, Socal, Gulf, and Texaco, and CFP also entered into the agreement. Between 1930 and 1934 at least three inter-company agreements were signed, based on the Achnacarry Agreement. The three were the Memorandum on European Markets (1930), Principles for a Distribution Adjustment (December 1932), and the Draft Memorandum of Principles (June 1934).
9. On the East Texas episode and the control measures taken by the major oil

companies see John M. Blair, *The Control of Oil* (New York: Pantheon, 1976), p. 126, passim; Harvey O'Connor, *The Empire of Oil* (New York: Monthly Review Press, 1955), p. 17, passim.

10. Thierry de Montbrial, *Energie: le compte à rebours* (energy: the countdown), p. 216 (English-language translation published in New York by Pergamon Press, 1979).

11. Richard Nehring, *Giant Oil Fields and World Oil Resources* (Santa Monica, Cal.: Rand, June 1978). A study prepared for the Central Intelligence Agency.

12. Ibid., p. 61.

13. Edgar Wesley Owen, *Trek of the Oil Finders: A History of Exploration for Petroleum* (Tulsa, Okla.: American Association of Petroleum Geologists, 1975.)

14. *International Petroleum Cartel*, Report of the Federal Trade Commission to the U.S. Senate (Washington, D.C., 1952), p. 171ff.

15. On the topic see Blair, p. 165.

16. See Edith Penrose and E.F. Penrose, *Iraq: International Relations and National Development* (London: E. Benn, 1978), ch. 5, 6; Blair, p. 83; Robert Engler, *The Brotherhood of Oil: Energy Policy and the Public Interest* (Chicago: University of Chicago Press, 1977), p. 118.

17. Nurul Islam, "Economic Interdependence between Rich and Poor Nations," *Third World Quarterly* 3 (April 1981):234.

18. The changes in the international oil system since the Iranian Revolution have inspired a great deal of literature on the subject. See Pierre Terzian, "Les résultats financiers des nouveaux contrats d'exploration-production pétrolière dans les pays arabes et en Iran," *Le Pétrole et le gas arabes*, Paris, May 1, 1980; Shell Briefing Service *The Changing World of Oil Supply*, Rotterdam, June 1980; Jochen H. Mohnfeld, "Changing Patterns of Trade," *Petroleum Economist*, London, August 1980; Nordine Air Laoussine, "OPEC Oil: Recent Developments and Problems of Supply," paper presented to the Second Energy Seminar at Oxford (GB) in September 1980 and reproduced as a supplment to the *Middle East Economic Survey*, September 29, 1980. See also the successive issues of the *OPEC Review* (Vienna).

19. "BP to be Less Oily," report of the speech of Sir David Steel, *The Times,* London, April 13, 1981.

20. See Owen, p. 1233ff. Among American authors see Peter Seaborn Smith, *Petróleo e política no Brasil moderno* (oil and politics in modern Brazil) (Brasilia: University of Brasilia, 1978), ch. 1; Peter Evans, *A tríplice aliança* (the triple alliance) (Rio de Janeiro: Zahar, 1980), ch. 2.

21. See Gabriel Cohn, *Petróleo e Nacionalismo* (oil and nationalism) (Sao Paulo, 1968, p. 63.

22. It is not a question of the company's technical competence. Using the same personnel and technical resources it discovered the giant Majnun field in Iraq. Despite several years of work by the multinationals, under risk contracts, they have made no discoveries of commercial importance off the Brazilian coast. By the end of 1982, Petrobras had been able to raise Brazilian oil production to a record of 300 thousand B/D.

23. Peter R. Odell and Kenneth E. Rosing, *The Future of Oil* (New York: Nichols, 1980).

24. Ibid., p. 29, n 2.
25. The work of Bernardo F. Grossling has become well known through pub-
     lications and memoranda published by the Inter-American Development
     Bank and collections of papers delivered at international conferences. See
     Bernardo F. Grossling, "The Petroleum Exploration Challenge with Re-
     spect to Developing Nations," *The Future Supply of Nature-Made Petrole-
     um and Gas* (1st conference of UNITAR, Laxenburg, Austria, July 1976).
26. The various aspects of these World Bank programs were thoroughly
     examined at the UN Conference on Oil Development (The Hague, March
     1981).
27. A significant example of those very much needed innovations is the
     Trinational Oil Company, whose creation was accorded in between Brazil,
     Mexico, and Venezuela, by protocol signed in Caracas on October 16,
     1981. The act was signed by the energy ministers of the three coun-
     tries involved and by late 1982 had already been definitively
     approved by the corresponding instances of Brazil and Mexico. The
     approval of the Venezuelan Congress was being expected at any
     moment.
28. OPEC documents and writings show that to be the prevailing opinion of the
     organization. *OPEC Review* 5 (Summer 1981) includes several articles that
     coincide with the ideas developed here. See especially an article by the
     deputy secretary general of OPEC, Fadhil J. Al-Chalabi, "Problems of
     World Energy Transition: Producer's Point of View."

5
Trade Relations between Arab and Latin American Countries

Mohamad W. Khouja

The analysis of present and potential trade relations between two such broad regions as the Arab world and Latin America is a very difficult task indeed. The difficulty emanates not only from the arduousness of identifying the basic factors that govern such relations, but also from the great diversity to be found within each region. This diversity is manifested in a variety of aspects, among which resource endowments, stages of development, levels of income, and degrees of national self-sufficiency are of special significance within the context of this chapter. Therefore, while much aggregation is unavoidable, the results should be treated with caution, and generalizations with corresponding reserve. Attempts will often be made to classify the Arab countries into two groups: oil and nonoil. Since this convenient classification is not meaningful for the Latin American countries, they will be grouped according to the conventional criterion of per capita income.

The Arab World

The Arab World is a geographic expanse which extends from the Arabian peninsula to the African shores of the Atlantic Ocean. It includes a total of twenty-one countries, of which only seven are considered major net exporters of oil, with some five more gradually increasing in importance as oil producers. They may be classified as in Table 5.1, which shows that in 1977 the Arab countries had a total population of approximately 148 million and a combined GNP of about $150 billion. Per capita GNP ranges from a low of $100 in the case of Somalia to a high of about $12,000 for Kuwait and the United Arab Emirates. (Appendix 5.1 contains more details on individual countries.) To put things in perspective, the Arab world has an area over twelve times that of France, three times its population, and about half its GNP.

59

In aggregate, it has immense economic power, producing about 60 percent of the free world's oil and controlling foreign financial assets worth almost $200 billion. With its control of approximately two-thirds of the oil reserves of the free world, and possessing vast agricultural lands capable of greatly increased production, the potential power of the Arab world is even greater than it is at present.

TABLE 5.1
Classification of the Arab Countries (1976)

	Number of Countries	Population (million)	GNP ($ billion)
Oil countries	7	41	94
Non-oil countries	14	104	46
(of which)			
Low income (incl. Djibouti)	(7)	(67)	(20)
Medium income	(4)	(33)	(20)
High income	(3)	(4)	(6)
Total	21	145	140

Regarding external trade, the rise in the value of Arab imports and exports since 1973 has been enormous. Total commodity exports increased in 1973–76 from about $26 billion to about $87 billion, nearly 235 percent. This is equivalent to an annual growth rate of more than 75 percent, more than three times the corresponding growth rate of world exports during the same period (approximately 21 percent annually). As shown in Table 5.2, the bulk of the increase is due to the exports of the oil countries, which accounted for over 90 percent of total Arab exports during 1973–76. Exports of nonoil countries increased in 1973–74, but declined slightly from then onward.

Similar changes are observed on the import side, where the total increased from about $15.5 billion in 1973 to almost $47 billion in 1976, a growth of more than 200 percent or 67 percent annually. Although the share of the seven oil countries in total imports is markedly lower than their corresponding share in exports, they are still predominant with their

TABLE 5.2
Evolution of Arab Trade ($ billions)

	EXPORTS				IMPORTS			
	1973	1974	1975	1976	1973	1974	1975	1976
Oil Countries	21.9	70.3	66.6	81.8	9.6	18.5	27.8	33.8
Share of Total	83.9%	92.3%	92.0%	93.7%	61.9%	68.3%	69.8%	72.4%
Other Countries	4.2	5.9	5.8	5.5	5.9	8.6	12.0	12.9
Share of Total	16.1%	7.7%	8.0%	6.3%	38.1%	31.7%	30.2%	27.6%
Total	26.1	76.2	72.4	87.3	15.5	27.1	39.8	46.7

Source: A. Al-Hamad, *Arabian Markets and Arabian Development* (Kuwait: Kuwait Fund for Arab Economic Development, 1977).

imports increasing by about 84 percent annually compared with a 30 percent annual increase in the imports of the nonoil countries.

Latin America

Latin America covers a vast land mass, and to consider it as a single entity involves even greater abstraction than in the case of the Arab world. In terms of area it is about double the size of the latter, with a total population of approximately 325 million in 1976, a little more than double that of the Arab world. The combined GNP of the entire area is in the order of $330 billion or roughly 120 percent more than the corresponding figure for the Arab countries. Although it is difficult to determine exactly which countries constitute Latin America, we have regarded all countries in Central and South America as falling under that heading. According to the 1977 World Bank Atlas this would imply a total of forty-one countries. Fifteen of these have populations of less than 300,000, and include a few island countries that have not yet become fully independent. Our discussion will be confined to the twenty-five countries that appear in Appendix 2 plus Cuba. The total population of these countries is in the order of 315 million, and for the purposes of this analysis they have been classified according to per capita GNP into the three categories given in Table 5.3.

The evolution of Latin American external trade has been far less dramatic than that of the Arab countries. As shown in Table 5.4, in 1974–77 exports increased by about 25 percent or at an average annual

TABLE 5.3
Classification of Latin American Countries* (1976)

Per Capita GNP	Number of Countries	Population (Million)	GNP ($ Billion)
Less than $ 750	9	75	44
$ 750 - $ 1100	8*	111	120
More than $ 1100	9	129	166
Total	26*	315	330

*Including Cuba

rate of 8 percent. Correspondingly, imports increased during the same period by about 40 percent, or at an average annual rate of nearly 13 percent. The highest rates of increase are observed in the exports of low-income countries and in the imports of high-income countries whose proportion of Latin American exports and imports increased respectively from 15 to 19 percent and from 51 to 57 percent.

TABLE 5.4
Evolution of Latin American Trade ($ billions)

Country group according to GNP per capita	EXPORTS				IMPORTS			
	1974	1975	1976	1977	1974	1975	1976	1977
Less than $ 750	6.4	6.0	6.8	9.7	6.4	7.8	7.8	10.4
Share of total	15%	16%	16%	19%	16%	15%	16%	18%
$ 750 - $ 1100	10.8	9.2	10.5	13.9	13.5	14.0	11.3	14.4
Share of total	26%	24%	24%	27%	33%	28%	24%	25%
Over $ 1100	24.1	23.1	26.0	27.9	21.2	28.5	29.6	32.3
Share of total	59%	60%	60%	54%	51%	57%	60%	57%
Total	41.3	38.3	43.3	51.5	41.1	50.3	48.7	57.1

Source: International Monetary Fund (IMF), *Direction of Trade, 1971-1977.* IMF, *International Financial Statistics.* Various issues.

Major Characteristics of the Foreign Trade Sectors

The two groups of countries have a number of distinct characteristics in regard to foreign trade,[1] and these may be summarized as follows.

The Arab Region

1. A high degree of dependence on foreign trade. Measured in terms of the ratio of exports plus imports to GDP, the degree of dependence on foreign trade exceeds 50 percent in almost all Arab countries and 100 percent in such oil-exporting countries as Saudi Arabia, Kuwait, Libya, Qatar, and the United Arab Emirates. In the latter group it is not only a case of high dependence on foreign trade, but also a case in which imports exceed the value of goods and services produced to meet local demand. This characteristic, along with high levels of income, indicates the importance of these countries as an import market.
2. A high degree of export concentration in most Arab countries, particularly the oil-exporting. This concentration has become intense in such countries as Iraq, Syria, Egypt, and Saudi Arabia, where efforts to diversify exports in recent years have been more successful. In Kuwait, Algeria, Qatar, and the United States Emirates oil exports have assumed greater prominence and the degree of concentration remains high.
3. The marginal propensity to import is high in low-income countries, which belong mainly to the non–oil-exporting group. Oil-exporting countries have a low marginal propensity to spend, due to an exceedingly high per capita income in most countries in this group. Some of these countries have a low absorptive capacity, and consequently Kuwait, Saudi Arabia, and Libya have marginal propensities to import estimated at 0.16, 0.25, and 0.37 respectively. While the marginal propensities to import may be low, the average income levels are very high, and Arab oil-exporting countries have reached per capita import levels that exceed those of most industrial countries. These characteristics indicate the importance of foreign trade for the Arab countries generally and the oil-exporting countries in particular. They also emphasize the vulnerability of these countries to external trade—an aspect of extreme significance in terms of trade development with new trading partners.
4. There is heavy concentration of food products, consumer goods, transport equipment, and construction materials among Arab imports. Intermediate goods, industrial raw materials, and heavy machinery are less prominent, due in part to the low absorptive capacity of most of those with a high per capita income.

Latin America

1. Although Latin American countries share with the Arab countries many developmental problems, their foreign trade displays many characteristics quite unlike those of the Arab world. Foremost among them is the relatively low dependence of the Latin American countries on foreign trade. Of the seven largest Latin American countries, Brazil, Argentina, Mexico, Colombia, Peru, Chile, and Venezuela, only the latter has a ratio of trade to GDP of more than 50 percent (54 percent). The other countries have a ratio that ranges from a low of 15 percent in the case of Mexico to a high of 30 percent in the case of Peru. This shows the importance of indigenous production in meeting domestic demand and the high degree of self-sufficiency enjoyed by these countries along with other sizable countries in Latin America.
2. Export concentration varies greatly among Latin American countries, but it is generally lower than that of Arab countries. It is highest in such primary producing countries as Colombia, Costa Rica, Guatemala, El Salvador, Ecuador, and Venezuela. Export concentration is low in the bigger and more diversified economies such as Brazil, Argentina, and to a lesser extent Mexico. Coffee, sugar, and fruits are the major export products for these countries, except Ecuador and Venezuela, which are important exporters of crude petroleum.
3. As in the case of developing countries under similar conditions, and in contrast to many Arab countries, the marginal propensity to import is high in most Latin American countries. Unlike many Arab countries, Latin American countries have a high marginal propensity to spend because of their lower income levels. In view of this, their imports per capita are substantially lower than those in most Arab countries, particularly the Arab oil-exporting states.
4. The composition of Latin American imports is considerably different from that in Arab countries. Food products, construction materials, and transport equipment are less prominent among Latin American imports, and there is greater balance in their overall composition than in the case of Arab imports.

Intraregional Trade

Intraregional trade in the Arab world is still very limited despite institutional efforts aimed at facilitating and expanding it. This trade represents about 5 percent of the total foreign trade of these countries. Intraregional trade among Latin American countries is considerably more important. Its ratio to the area's total foreign trade is estimated at more than double that of the Arab world. Although this will later be considered in greater detail, the main reason for higher regional trade in Latin America seems to be in the broader natural resource base and greater diversity of geographic and climatic conditions in that continent than in the Arab region. While the Arab world occupies a band covering a quarter of a circle of the globe, it is confined largely between 10 and 30° N, whereas Latin America stretches from 30° N across the Equator and down almost to Antarctica. In addition, the disparity of economic conditions among Latin American countries contributes significantly toward promotion and expansion of this trade. None of these factors are as prominent in the case of the Arab region.

Record of Trade Relations between the Two Groups

Trade relations between the Arab world and Latin America have been limited in volume, country distribution, and composition. Total Arab exports to Latin American countries in 1969–76 totaled about $20 billion, representing 4.8 percent of total Arab exports for those years. Arab imports were even more modest, amounting during the same period to less than $3 billion, or about 1.5 percent of total Arab imports. Latin American exports to the Arab world represent approximately 8 percent of their total exports for 1969–76, and their corresponding imports about 1.3 percent. As shown in Appendix 3, Latin American countries rank fifth in relative importance among regions that import from the Arab world, with Western Europe occupying first place followed by Asia, the Eastern Block, and North America. Among regions that export to the Arab world, the Latin American countries rank sixth, followed only by Africa and Oceania. Similarly, the Arab countries rank fairly low among Latin American trading partners. This aggregation should not be allowed to conceal the large amount of trade that takes place between some countries in both groups. Brazil, Argentina, and Uruguay, for example, have important trade relations with a number of oil-exporting countries. These three countries accounted in 1977 for more than 90 percent of Latin American exports to, and 88 percent of their imports from, the Arab world. Similarly, the Arab oil-exporting countries account for 97 percent of Arab exports to, and over 55 percent of their imports from, Latin America. The reason for this lopsided distribution is due to the pattern of trade between the two groups. A major part of the oil needs of Brazil and Argentina is satisfied through imports from Arab oil-exporting countries—Saudi Arabia, Libya, Iraq, and Kuwait. Correspondingly, these four countries along with such countries as Syria,

Lebanon, and Egypt, which have had historical ties with latin America, are traditional importers of food products and consumer goods from Brazil, Argentina, Uruguay, and Panama.

Apart from the lopsidedness in the distribution of trade and its product concentration, trade relations between the two groups have been characterized by a substantial trade surplus in favor of the Arab countries, estimated in 1977 at more than $3.5 billion. This surplus has been increasing considerably in the last few years following the rise of oil prices in 1973 and 1974. When considered on an individual country basis rather than as two large groups of countries, we find that fourteen Latin American countries had trade surpluses with Arab countries in 1977 compared with eight countries having trade deficits. The former group includes such countries as Colombia, Guatemala, Ecuador, the Dominican Republic, Peru, Chile, Mexico, and Costa Rica. The deficit group consists primarily of Brazil, Panama, and Argentina. Of the twenty Arab countries that have trade relations with Latin America, eight, almost all oil-exporting countries, have had trade surpluses and the rest trade deficits.

The great majority of both Latin American and Arab countries have enjoyed some trade with countries from the other group. In spite of the limited volume of trade which has so far taken place, it seems obvious that trade channels and links have been established which need to be further strengthened and developed. Although institutional links are of great importance in international trade, they can only play a major role if certain economic conditions for the existence and promotion of trade are present. It is to the economic factors that govern such relations among countries and determine their potential that we now turn.

Basic Economic Conditions

Differences in resource endowments, factor intensities, and patterns of production and consumption are considered the main causes for differences in comparative costs among countries, and it is these comparative costs which form the basis of international trade relations. Such basic differences account for various degrees of complementarity in the economic structures of different countries, which in turn determine the extent of trade that can potentially take place among them. In view of the observed similarities among many Arab and Latin American countries, it is not surprising to see the modest level of trade relations described earlier. Both groups are net importers of manufactured goods, heavy industrial machinery, and transport equipment. In addition, whereas many Latin American countries are important producers of industrial raw materials, the majority of Arab countries are in a stage of development at which their demand for such goods is minimal. Although the picture regarding factor endowment is appreciably different, particularly regarding the oil-exporting countries, the relative abundance of capital in many Arab countries has not yet been reflected in their structures and production patterns. Correspondingly, a number of Arab countries enjoy relative abundance of labor similar to that of many Latin American countries. With such limited complementarity in basic economic conditions, differences in comparative costs are unlikely to be sufficiently large to offset high transport costs and increased competition from other markets which are more accessible either to the Arab world or to Latin America.

Prospects for Trade Expansion

In spite of the aforementioned limitations, a number of prospects for expanding trade relations between Arab and Latin American countries should be emphasized.[2] Foremost among them is an increase in trade in food products. With the Arab world being far from self-sufficient in foodstuffs, its net import requirements could largely be satisfied through the exceptional productive capacity of many Latin American countries. This is particularly true in the case of grains, sugar, meat, and vegetable oils, all of which the Arab countries regularly import in large quantities. Correspondingly, the abundant oil reserves of the Arab countries provide the basis for such expansion of trade through their ability to meet the import requirements of Latin America in crude oil, fertilizers, and other petrochemical products. Many Latin American countries have developed an efficient contracting capability and could play a major role in alleviating the construction problems of many Arab countries. A noticeable measure of success has already been achieved in this field by some Brazilian contractors who have become well established in a number of Arab countries. These areas of trade should be further developed by the promotion of institutions and channels of business communication facilitating trade relations between the two groups helping overcome the problems of distance and lack of familiarity each has with the business practices of the other.

As well as the prospects mentioned above, trade relations between the two groups could expand to cover other primary commodities including raw materials and a range of manufactured goods. Imports of raw materials to the Arab countries are increasing rapidly with the pace of industrial progress. The scope of this trade is substantial, as evidenced by the setting up of aluminum and steel plants in the Arabian Gulf and other parts of the Arab world, or raw materials supplied from such far away places as West Africa and Australia. The establishment of such large-scale processing operations with their high-energy cost components and capital intensity is expected to accelerate as the Arab oil-producing countries pursue their aim of developing their production base in accordance with their resource endowment. Given the scarcity of such industrial raw materials as bauxite, copper, and other metal ores in the Arab countries, Latin America could emerge as a major supplier of these materials to the Arab world on a secure and long-term basis. The Latin American countries could also become an important source of such construction materials as lumber, steel, and cement, the demand for which has been steadily increasing with the rise in income of Arab oil-producing countries and the implementation of large housing and other construction programs throughout the Arab world.

The Arab countries would similarly expect to expand their export of products other than crude oil. Although the range of such products is at present limited, many Arab countries are in need of markets for their expanding petrochemical industries and phosphate mining operations. Export of these products could be expanded to the mutual benefit of both groups of countries. While trade could be expanded in both directions, it should be recognized that there is a greater need to increase Latin American exports to the Arab world to eliminate the imbalance referred to earlier. This should not pose any serious problems in view of the great export potential of Latin American countries. This potential may be exploited more rapidly through joint ventures in either service activities designed to facilitate the flow of goods between the two groups or in mining and processing operations that require capital investment presently unavailable in Latin America. Arab oil-producing countries could provide the latter in the form of complete and integrated packages suited to the recipient's needs.

Expansion of trade in manufactured goods is a high priority for countries in both groups, particularly as they attempt to make full use of their resources and join the ranks of industrialized countries. Establishment of joint ventures in this field of activity would secure supplies and markets for the countries concerned and would develop stronger and more stable relations between them. With the capital resources of Arab oil-producing countries, Latin American supplies of raw materials, and the joint markets of the two groups of countries, many manufacturing industries could be viable and operate on an efficient and competitive basis. Joint ventures could be developed in many sectors without, as some argue, the need to invite the participation of the more developed countries. The two groups would be able to provide, on their own, the various inputs required to execute projects in a broad range of manufacturing industries. Even medium and heavy industries could be established with the financial resources, technical know-how, and primary inputs presently available. It is true that more sophisticated industries requiring advanced technologies and patented processes of production may not be viable without the cooperation of participants from developed countries. Also, third-party participation might be necessary in some instances to ensure suitable markets beyond that of the combined Arab world and Latin America. In the short run, priority should be given to projects seeking to satisfy local demand for essential products in countries of the two groups and to surmounting problems of marketing and availibility of raw materials through promotion of joint ventures. This form of cooperation would not only be mutually beneficial, but also a two-way concern, for in their strenuous efforts to diversify their economies and promote industrialization, Arab oil-producing countries need the cooperation of Latin American countries to help them ensure a steady supply of raw materials and to secure markets for their products.

Another area of possible cooperation in trade-related activities is concerned with the pricing of primary commodities which would play an important part if the production possibilities of many of the countries in both groups were developed. Arab countries with sufficient financial means could assist in creating and financing international stocks of such commodities to protect and stabilize their prices. If this concept were properly developed it could also facilitate the investment of part of the financial resources of Arab oil-producing countries in a manner that would protect against currency devaluation and thus safeguard their real value. There is obviously a mutual benefit to be reaped from such a broad commodity stabilization scheme. Most Arab countries, and the oil-producing countries in particular, have expressed support for the UNCTAD (United Nations Conference on Trade and Development) sponsored common fund for primary commodities and have indicated their preparedness to participate in it. The proposed fund would be improved if appropriate means were available to protect the real value of investments in commodity stocks by those countries presently holding financial surpluses. World trade generally could only benefit by such improvement.

Conclusion

Trade relations among developing countries are often limited because of the high degree of similarity in their production patterns. In spite of differences in potential, this observation is largely valid in the case of Arab and Latin American countries. Trade expansion between the two groups would require efforts to diversify their production bases and reduce export concentration. This can only be achieved by a long-term process and requires a greater measure of transformation than has thus far been possible in most developing countries. Given the basic differences in factor and resource endowments of the two regions, the prospects for trade expansion are nonetheless significant. This is especially true of the financial resources of the Arab world, the raw materials available in Latin American countries, and the combined markets of the two regions. Such ventures would aim at the efficient use of resource endowments of the two regions and would provide the needed incentives to facilitate marketing and promote mutual trade.

Appropriate channels and institutions should also be developed to further Arab–Latin American trade relations. Some progress has already been achieved in the creation of joint chambers of commerce and banking operations. There is considerable scope for developing new channels and the establishment of more trade promotion organizations in the two regions. Such developments should also cover expanding shipping and air transport services and the provision of resident trade missions.

The benefits of trade expansion are well known, but they would achieve particular importance in the context of Arab–Latin American trade because of the special factors discussed in this paper. Given the aspirations of the people of both regions to achieve improved living conditions and sustained growth, no efforts should be spared to reap those benefits to the fullest extent, as both regions constitute an integral part of the Third World whose progress depends largely on economic cooperation and political solidarity among its members.

Notes

I wish to express my appreciation to Peter G. Sadler, Director, Institute for the Study of Sparsely Populated Areas, for reading and making invaluable comments and suggestions on the final draft of this chapter.

1. These characteristics are based primarily on empirical evidence reported in A. Sadik, "Special Characteristics of Foreign Trade for Some Members of OAPEC," *Journal of Oil and Gas Cooperation* 4(1978): 107-17.
2. The following discussion is based in part on my paper "Towards a Strategy for Economic Cooperation between the Arab Oil Producing Countries and the Third World," *Masga Quarterly Journal* 4(1977): 1-18.

APPENDIX 5.1
Arab Countries:* Population, GNP, and Foreign Trade (1976)

	Population ('000)	GNP ($ million)	GNP ($ per capita)	Imports ($ million)	Exports ($ million)	Imports ($ per capita)	Exports to LA ($ million)	Imports from LA ($ million)
Oil Countries								
1. Algeria	16,250	13,250	810	5,604	5,094	336	58.5	191.3
2. Iraq	11,500	15,400	1,340	3,863	10,377	364	1112.3	24.8
3. Saudi Arabia	8,000	27,700	3,200	13,266	44,574	1,470	3376.0	21.0
4. Libya	2,540	13,720	5,390	5,221	8,879	1,479	500.4	64.7
5. Qatar	220	1,960	8,940	1,058	2,407	3,713	258.7	0.7
6. UAE	770	8,750	11,400	3,918	9,331	3,928	395.9	12.4
7. Kuwait	1,050	12,400	11,750	4,332	10,861	2,800	16.0	301.0
Non-oil Countries								
A. Low Income								
1. Somalia	3,250	330	100	193	125	48	6.1	2.8
2. North Yemen	6,500	1,400	210	542	10	63	-	0.2
3. South Yemen	1,725	400	230	296	313	208	0.1	2.17
4. Sudan	16,000	4,800	300	1,116	663	61	4.2	14.8
5. Egypt	38,000	12,000	310	5,425	2,396	93	29.1	112.6
6. Mauritania	1,350	430	310	252	192	141	-	8.9
B. Medium Income								
1. Jordan	2,800	1,300	470	1,069	244	330	-	5.41
2. Morocco	17,828	8,300	490	3,073	1,349	149	36.8	108.2
3. Syria	7,236	5,230	630	2,567	1,094	311	-	20.9
4. Tunisia	5,750	4,550	790	1,582	825	266	6.9	36.4
C. High Income								
1. Bahrain	270	780	2,900	1,843	1,552	3,600	1.0	3.4
2. Oman	790	1,950	2,460	758	1,638	225	-	-
3. Lebanon	3,250	3,500	1,080	977	968	427	19.3	5.3

Source: A. Al-Hamad, Arabian Markets and Arabian Development (Kuwait : Kuwait Fund for Arab Economic Development, 1977) p. 15; and IMF Direction of Foreign Trade.

*Excluding Djibouti

APPENDIX 5.2
Latin American Countries: Population, GNP, and Foreign Trade

Country	Population (million) (1976)	GNP ($ million) (1976)	GNP ($ per capita) (1976)	Imports ($ million) (1977)	Exports ($ million) (1977)	Imports ($ per capita) (1977)	Exports to Arab World ($ thousand) (1977)	Imports from Arab World ($ thousand) (1977)
Per Capita GNP ≤ $ 750								
Haiti	4.67	1,159	248	358	225	76	50	–
Honduras	2.83	1,210	428	576	504	192	–	–
Bolivia	5.79	2,905	502	831	537	143	–	40
El Salvador	4.12	2,179	529	885	1,220	216	480	30
Guyana	0.78	461	581	311	281	389	20,940	–
Columbia	24.33	14,343	590	2,299	2,462	95	13,130	300
Paraguay	2.78	1,671	601	309	279	119	2,090	23,480
Guatemala	6.26	4,294	686	1,144	1,156	176	6,800	400
Peru	15.91	10,931	687	1,934	1,547	122	7,400	–
Ecuador	7.31	5,059	692	1,704	1,477	233	3,800	–
Per Capita GNP $ 750 – $1100								
Chile	10.45	8,172	782	2,259	2,036	215	12,400	–
Dominican Republic	4.84	3,791	783	985	779	203	16,300	–
Nicaragua	2.23	1,786	801	772	696	336	1,590	30
Mexico	62.33	61,193	982	5,486	4,168	89	8,200	900
Uruguay	3.76*	3,004*	982*	730	608	261	30,530	112,630
a) Argentina	25.58*	26,347*	1,030*	4,200	5,627	163	118,700	153,900
Per Capita GNP > $1100								
Brazil	109.2	124,196	1,137	13,193	12,137	120	482,000	3,359,000
Costa Rica	2.02	2,339	1,159	999	789	495	1,200	2,750
Panama	1.72	2,006	1,166	1,709	243	1,005	890	74,330
Jamaica	2.07	2,455	1,186	713	617	344	–	–
Surinam	0.44	515	1,170	385	331	917	1,700	–
Barbados	0.25	379	1,516	273	95	910	–	–
Trinidad & Tobago	1.10	2,454	2,240	1,789	2,176	1,626	100	10
Venezuela	12.36	31,105	2,517	9,861	9,734	795	2,000	16,000
Bahamas	0.20*	641	3,110*	3,387	1,767	16,442	–	10

* = 1975 figures

a) Due to hyperinflation, GNP and GNP per capita have been interpolated from best data available to be consistent with the rest of the table.

Source: IMF Direction of Trade, Annual 1971-1977
       IMF International Financial Statistics, November 1978.

APPENDIX 5.3
Geographic Distribution of Arab Foreign Trade (1969-76)

$ Billion

	Oil Countries				Non-Oil Countries				All Arab Countries			
	Exports	%	Imports	%	Exports	%	Imports	%	Exports	%	Imports	%
North America	26.5	7.5	15.7	12.3	1.5	3.7	6.7	9.9	28.4	7.1	22.5	11.4
South America	19.5	5.4	1.6	1.2	0.4	1.1	1.3	1.9	19.9	4.8	2.9	1.5
Europe	147.9	41.0	55.0	43.0	15.8	39.6	31.4	45.8	163.6	40.9	86.3	44.0
Africa	2.9	0.8	0.7	0.4	0.5	1.3	1.0	1.5	3.4	0.9	1.6	0.9
Asia	65.3	18.1	21.1	16.5	2.3	5.9	5.1	7.5	67.7	16.9	26.2	13.4
Arab Countries	8.7	2.4	10.3	8.1	5.9	14.9	5.3	7.7	14.6	3.6	15.6	8.0
Australia, New Zealand	3.7	1.0	1.3	1.0	0.1	0.4	1.1	1.5	3.9	1.0	2.3	1.2
Communist Countries	32.9	9.1	6.6	5.2	8.3	21.0	8.7	12.8	41.2	10.3	15.4	7.8
Others	52.8	14.6	15.6	12.2	4.8	12.1	7.9	11.5	57.6	14.4	23.5	12.0
Total	360.7	100.0	127.9	100.0	39.7	100.0	68.5	100.0	400.0	100.0	196.2	100.0

Source: Kuwait Fund for Arab Economic Development, Geographical Distribution of Arab Foreign Trade, December 1977

6

Financial Cooperation between the Arab World and Latin America: The Role of the Inter-American Development Bank

Armando Prugue

The historical formation of Latin America has been influenced by Islamic thought, not only as a corollary of the Iberian origins of its nations but also more recently, as a result of growing participation by descendants of immigrants from Arab countries in the political, economic, and cultural life of Latin America. In addition, increasing cooperation between Latin American and Arab countries is the result of a mutual awareness of the common linkages between developing countries and the complementarity between the economies of many of the nations in both regions.

Throughout the Western Hemisphere, in virtually every country south of the Rio Grande and in every field of endeavor, there are distinguished leaders who have blended into the Latin American culture while remaining proud of their Arab heritage. At the level of intergovernmental relations, there has been a professed solidarity between the two regions in all pertinent international forums. There is also a very active exchange of diplomatic and trade missions which bears witness to the burgeoning relationships between the Arab world and Latin America.

The financial component of this relationship is an essential ingredient in the concept of economic cooperation among developing countries. Interest in such cooperation has been evident long before the surplus of petrodollars in OPEC countries made their capitals the favorite rendezvous of the Western financial community. The fact that Latin America, as an area comprising most middle-income developing countries, has acquired sufficient experience in its access to the world money markets to finance huge development projects, has not been lost in Arab statesmen, who have for many years taken interest in Latin America's pragmatic approach to development financing.

One of the areas in which Latin American experience is especially germane to Arab needs and expectations is that of institutional development of financial agencies, whether capitalized from public, private, or mixed sources. These agencies differ from commercial banking because of the medium to long-term range of their financing and the developmental nature of their operations. There are now between 250 and 400 such development financing institutions in Latin America, the majority of which were established within the last twenty years. Their activities are monitored by ALIDE—the Latin American Association of Development Financing Institutions, an organization headquartered in Lima, Peru—which has been performing invaluable services for the region and should be willing to collaborate with related institutions in the Arab world.

When one considers the entire panorama of financial cooperation between the Arab world and Latin America, it is necessary to distinguish two basic aspects: that related to international financial institutions, and that pertaining to contacts between purely national entities, whether public or private. The leading international financial institution in Latin America is the Inter-American Development Bank (IDB), whose level of operations for the region, exceeding 2.5 billion in loans per annum, approximates that of the World Bank.

The IDB was established in 1959 by twenty countries of the Western Hemisphere, both developed (the United States) and developing (nineteen Latin American nations). As decolonization proceeded in the Caribbean, a number of newly sovereign nations from the area gradually joined the bank, as did Canada in 1972, and the institution thus became the first genuinely regional development bank, followed shortly after its inception by similar financial agencies in Africa, Asia, and the Middle East, and by a number of subregional development banks throughout Latin America and the rest of the developing world. In 1976 and 1977, a total of fifteen nations from outside the Western Hemisphere—mostly from Europe and Japan—also joined the Inter-American Development Bank as full-fledged members, thus bringing the total of shareholder governments to forty-three, but without prejudice to the institution's original commitment "to contribute to the acceleration of the process of economic and social development of the regional developing member countries (i.e., Latin America, which includes the Caribbean) individually and collectively."

The IDB greatly benefited at the outset of its activities from assistance provided by the World Bank in terms of initial operating policies and procedures, which were adapted to the needs and requirements of a regional development financing institution placing emphasis on the social and economic aspects of development. In turn, the experience of the IDB was made available to other financial institutions which emerged in the Third World. The newest of these is the Islamic Development Bank, created in 1974, with which the IDB maintains a close and continuing collaboration, as well as with the Asian and African development banks and a number of subregional and national institutions on other continents.

Contacts between the IDB and the Arab world were initiated by the first president of the bank, Felipe Herrera, from Chile. Upon assuming the direction of the bank in 1971 the new president, Antonio Ortiz Mena, made a point of pursuing and improving such contacts through several personal visits to Arab capitals and other means. In his former capacity as Mexico's minister of finance he had maintained over the years excellent personal and functional relationships with many distinguished Arab financiers, and in the course of various international monetary and other gatherings he became acutely aware of the underlying similarity of situations and aspirations between Latin American countries, several of which are also oil producers, and those of the Middle East. This personal conviction as well as the cordial ties Ortiz Mena had developed led him to cultivate an institutional cooperative relationship on behalf of the IDB and its counterparts in the Arab world.

The rationale for this cooperation is the common commitment of Arab and Latin American countries to development, perceived as economic growth plus a measure of social justice sufficient to enable all the people to enjoy the fruits of such growth. Today, Arab leaders and statemen, as well as those responsible for the governments of the countries of Latin America and the Caribbean, regardless of their particular political persuasions, are united in placing priority on the promotion of the collective well-being of their peoples and the enhancement of the quality of their lives. It is therefore only natural that Latin America should share its own experience in this regard with other nations sharing these goals.

The uniqueness of the regional development banks stems from various elements, among which looms large the fact that, by virtue of their close interaction with the nations they serve, these banks can be particularly responsive to the needs and aspirations of a given region. Another factor lies in the possibilities which such regional institutions offer for improved mutual assistance and coordination among developing countries, thereby heightening their responsibilities and self-determination. Given the dwindling flow of official development assistance from traditional donor countries, it is imperative that developing nations foster their economic cooperation in the financial and technical domain, for which the regional banks, predicated as they are upon the solidarity of nations, provide the appropriate conduits.

Starting from the premise that aid delayed is aid denied, the OPEC countries have moved swiftly to provide relief to oil-importing developing countries whose economic growth has been stymied by the increase in oil prices in 1973 and 1979. As evidence of the kinship linking developing countries in general, and of the willingness of OPEC members to share their wealth with the most distressed nations in particular, both within and outside the Arab community, a whole panoply of new financial institutions funded by the resources of oil-exporting countries has sprung up, and joined older institutions that have been created in the Middle East to bring the benefits of modernization and development to all peoples.

A growing number of these financial institutions have either initiated or pursued operations in Latin America, some of them in cooperation with the Inter-American Development Bank. Two Latin American countries, Ecuador and Venezuela, are active members of OPEC, and the latter country—which has devised some of the most creative formulas to recycle its petrodollar surplus for the benefit of others within the Latin American region—is also a contributor to the OPEC fund. This fund is designed to strengthen financial cooperation among developing nations outside of OPEC through the provision of financial assistance.

The OPEC Fund for International Development (formerly the OPEC Special Fund) has been active in cofinancing projects with the IDB. To date nine such operations have been approved, totaling over $40 million in OPEC fund commitments, for projects as diverse as fisheries in the Dominican Republic; water, sewage, and sanitation in Bolivia, Haiti, and Paraguay; and hydroelectric power in Bolivia, Costa Rica, El Salvador, and Honduras. Other projects are being considered in Bolivia, Costa Rica, El Salvador, Guyana, Haiti, Honduras, Jamaica, Peru, and Panama.

Two other loans, involving cofinancing with the Saudi Fund for Economic and Social Development have also been negotiated, both loans pertain to hydroelectric power projects, one in Ecuador and one in Brazil, and the latter has been implemented. In the case of the Brazilian project, an agreement was signed in December 1977 whereby the Saudi fund committed US $55 million for transmission lines serving the Northeast of the country, while the bank was authorized to lend US $97.7 million for the project, deemed of critical importance for the development of Brazil. The IDB is willing and prepared to expand considerably its cofinancing operations, which should be of interest to financiers in the Arab world. The bank takes a flexible and pragmatic approach to these operations, including the possibility of establishing trust funds and other innovative formulas to mobilize external resources and harness them to Latin American development needs and priorities.

Brazil has been especially active in associating itself with Arab capital sources in a variety of bilateral ventures. For instance, it participated in a consortium with Kuwait investment sources in a 50/50 partnership for the formation of Arab-Brazilian Investment Co. headquarted in Brazil. Also, the Bank of Brazil is a shareholder in other joint ventures such as Banque Arabe et Internationale d'Investissement (BAII), established in 1973, and Kuwait Pacific Finance Co., founded in 1975. An Iraqi-Brazilian Bank was formed in 1981. The Libyan Arab Foreign Bank teamed up with Argentine capital to form a Libyan Argentine Investment Bank, and with a variety of other sources, both Arab and Latin American, to form a new Arab Latin American Bank (ARLABANK) with headquarters in Lima, Peru.

ARLABANK provides an example of concrete opportunities for cooperation among developing countries without prejudice to traditional merchant banking criteria. Bringing together the resources of ten Arab and seventeen Latin American financial institutions under the authority of a board of directors where no less than fourteen nationalities are represented, ARLABANK is a bold venture in Arab–Latin American cooperation. Founded in October 1977 with a fully subscribed capital of US $100 million (of which half is paid up—60 percent held by the Arab, and 40 percent by Latin American shareholders), the bank was designed as a bridge between the economies of the two regions. Incorporated under Peruvian law as an offshore multinational bank, ARLABANK's initial efforts are directed to international trade finance, project loans, and investment banking, as well as transactions in the Euromarkets, management and participation in international loan syndications, and the underwriting and management of capital issues in the Euromarkets. The bank has established an offshore unit at Manama, Bahrain, a representative office in London, and a regional office in Rio de Janeiro. Having initiated its operations in March 1978, net profits realized during the first fiscal year exceeded US $2.4 million.

The Inter-American Development Bank has for a long time cultivated excellent working and cooperative relationships with a number of Arab governments and their respective financial institutions. While none of these governments has joined the bank as a nonregional member, personal contacts between leading statesmen and financiers of the Arab world and directors and senior staff members of the IDB have established a framework for a close working relationship.

In Latin America as well as in the Middle East, no formal institutionalized cooperation can substitute for the personal trust upon which business relationships flourish. Hence the importance of reciprocal visits and a person-to-person approach. Many technical missions have been exchanged between the president, directors, and senior staff of the bank and financial institutions in the Arab countries, leading to better acquaintances and in some cases lasting friendships.

In September 1977 the IDB played host in Washington to the first meeting of regional development banks and other international development financing institutions. This meeting evidenced the closeness in our thinking and led to the exchange of project information which has proven mutually rewarding. In 1978 two IDB staff members cooperated with the Islamic Development Bank, at the latter's request, to assist its personnel at Jeddah in implementing appropriate operational procedures for this new institution. The IDB has also established a close collaboration with the International Fund for Agricultural Development (IFAD), which is a product of the development outlook and financial contributions of OPEC countries. To date eleven projects have been cofinanced, representing an IFAD commitment of nearly US $83 million, and another seven are under consideration for 1982.

At present the IDB maintains a close collaboration with five leading Arab financial institutions: the Islamic Development Bank, the Saudi Fund for Development, the Arab Fund for Economic and Social Development, the Abu Dhabi Fund for Arab Economic Development, and the Kuwaiti Fund for Arab Economic Development. The Board and staff of the IDB hope that they may soon enjoy the same satisfactory relationship with a wider array of institutions in the increasingly sophisticated Arab financial community.

A proposed colloquium on development financing and investment possibilities in developing countries, that would have convened in Algiers in 1975, could not ultimately be held. However, the president and officers of the IDB are confident that other opportunities will be found for such a gathering, which by bringing together financial experts from the Arab world and Latin America ought to contribute to a better mutual awareness of each others' needs and aspirations and to an exchange of ideas and experiences. I would advocate the extension of Arab–Latin American cooperation from the purely financial to a technical cooperation, where both regions face many common problems, which suggests the desirability of pooling their experiences in overcoming obstacles to development. In fields such as arid-land agriculture, irrigation, and the prevention of desertification, as well as a whole range of skills associated with petroleum and petrochemical industries, much more could be done by selective transfer and absorption of appropriate technology within the framework of Technical Cooperation among Developing Countries (TCDC) as discussed at the UN conference of August 1978 at Mar del Plata, Argentina. In other UN conferences covering the law of the sea, science and technology for development, and water, it has become quite apparent that here is an underlying affinity of interests between Arab and Latin American nations.

Latin American expertise and technology, developed in response to the challenges posed by the rugged nature of the region, are held in high esteem by Arab governments and entrepreneurs, who have awarded large public works contracts, won through competitive international bidding with multinational firms of worldwide renown, to Latin American engineering and consulting firms. From a road in Mauritania, oil drilling in Egypt and Iraq, airports in Saudi Arabia, to a design for a university in Algeria, and a variety of other mammoth projects, one finds the presence of Latin American skill, ingenuity, and creativity in large-scale works throughout Northern Africa and the Middle East. This bears witness not only to Latin America's technical skills and business acumen, but also to the underlying affinity which gives these business operations a pervasive human dimension, bringing to both peoples the benefits of development and modernization.

Although the IDB plays no direct role in this regard, since its own program for export promotion is both small and geographically restricted, the bank can render service to both Arab and Latin American countries in serving as a connecting bridge between their respective financial communities, without prejudice to existing and future bilateral relationships, both at official and private levels. In so doing, the IDB would be exploiting some unique features it shares with other regional development banks: an intimate contact with the nations it serves, an enviable repository of technical and financial expertise, and above all a commitment to both economic and social development without impairing its sound financial standing in the world's money markets.

The IDB can perform these functions vis-à-vis the Arab world in several mutually reinforcing ways. The first is to make its facilities available for channeling trust funds earmarked for Latin American development. Since 1961, when the United States established within the bank a Social Progress Trust Fund in the amount of US $525 million for the concessional financing of certain specified social development projects, until 1975, when Venezuela created a trust fund for the equivalent of half a billion dollars for other specified purposes, the bank has been charged with the administration of many such trust funds (amounting to over US $1.2 billion), including some from Canada,

France, the Holy See, Spain, Sweden, Switzerland, the United Kingdom, and other countries which subsequently became members of the bank.

Another form in which the IDB is prepared to place its facilities at the disposal of Arab governments desirous of contributing to development projects in Latin America—short of membership in the bank—is by associating itself with direct parallel loans and other cofinancing operations, some of which were cited earlier, as well as by permitting the purchase of shares in the bank's loan portfolios and assisting in the identification of direct investment possibilities. Other avenues for financial and technical cooperation may be identified, including IDB bond issues in Arab financial markets.

The IDB is seeking to develop mechanisms of mutual interest to donor and recipient countries, since enlightened self-interest is the best motivation for all governments to further the collective well-being of their peoples. The large body of financial expertise in both the Arab and Latin American financial communities ought to be tapped constructively to generate more creative ideas in this area. By working together we hope to be helpful to those leaders in both regions who visualize a partnership between the Arab and Latin American peoples, for their common good and the enhancement of the quality of their lives.

7

Toward a New Debate on "Recycling" Petrodollars in the 1980s

Fehmy Saddy

The World Bank's *World Development Report, 1981* begins its "Ten-Year Perspective" on the state of the world economy with this opening statement:

> The 1980s have begun on a sluggish note. Growth in the industrialized market economies as a group slowed down sharply in 1980 and will remain slow in 1981 as well. These countries show few signs of overcoming the inflationary legacy of the 1970s—just one of several similarities between two decades. Others include rising real oil prices; continuing large trade deficits and, consequently, heavy borrowing from abroad by the developing countries; and the prospect of much slower growth in low-income countries than in middle-income countries.[1]

With this perspective for the 1980s, the oil-exporting countries with some capital-surplus funds[2] find themselves in an unenviable position. Unable to cut their oil production, they will continue to face the problems they encountered in the 1970s in placing their capital-surplus funds in investments that preserve their real value. This goal has proven elusive due to inflation, currency depreciation, and sluggish economic growth in the industrialized countries. The rate of return on these investments in 1972–79 ranged between zero and -3.4 percent annually.[3] Prospects for better returns in the 1980s do not seem warranted, considering the structural problems that continue to afflict industrialized countries' economies. Inflation still seems uncontrollable, sluggish economy is characteristic of most of them, and social problems resulting from unemployment and stagnation are on the rise. This state of affairs has prompted a prominent economist to suggest that growth in industrialized countries will continue to be low in coming years as their economies undergo a cyclical decline. Recovery will ultimately come after structural adjustments are made, either by more efficient production or technological breakthroughs.[4]

The negative returns on investment of capital-surplus funds were not the only result of the "recycling" of petrodollars. The recycling strategy has had adverse effects on developing countries as well. One of these effects is the creation of a debt problem.[5] The debts of developing countries increased from $86.6 billion in 1971 to some $524 billion in 1981. This has placed a tremendous burden on these countries' ability to service this debt in coming years.[6]

The investment policies pursued by capital-surplus oil exporters have fallen within the general strategy of recycling. This strategy turned surpluses into debts to developing countries through the Western banking system. The economic results of this strategy were not only disadvantageous to both the capital-surplus and developing countries, but has also helped deepen the dependence of both on industrialized countries.

From its inception this strategy was oriented toward industrialized countries because of the adverse effects any curtailment of their growth would have on developing countries. This argument implied that what was good for the industrialized countries was good for the rest of the world. The recycling mechanism was structured for the purpose of helping the Western economies recover their strength. The experience of the last decade has proven the recycling strategy inadequate. Neither capital-surplus oil exporters nor oil-importing developing countries benefited from recycling: the former by deriving negative returns on their investments, the latter by increasing their indebtedness to an alarming level. The benefits that accrued to the industrialized countries were substantial, but they failed to bring about recovery for their economies, as they continue to face serious difficulties manifested in persistent stagflation, unemployment, and declining productivity. One analyst's comment on this state of affairs is that "economists' views about macro-economic theory and policy are in a greater state of disarray than at any time in living memory."[7]

In spite of the structural favoritism in the recycling strategy toward industrialized countries, achievements have been meager. Developing countries, which seem to have taken the brunt of recycling in the way of increased indebtedness, deterioration in trade terms, and curtailed exports, fared better. If this is any indication, it is that they are more viable economically and better candidates for future growth. Investment of capital surplus in these countries is at least as viable as in industrialized ones.

Developing countries maintained an average growth rate of 2.7 percent throughout the 1970s. This was higher than the average growth rate of 2.5 percent achieved by industrialized countries. The growth rate of some middle-income countries (MICs) reached higher levels than the average growth rate for all developing countries. The newly industrialized countries (NICs), particularly in East Asia and Latin America, demonstrated strong ability to withstand the world economic recession and maintained high levels of exports. On the whole, outward-looking countries in the Third World were willing to take the risk of heavy external borrowing to maintain their pace of development, and as a result they fared better than inward-looking countries. These countries are particularly viable for investment by capital-surplus oil exporters. Direct investment would help them reduce their borrowing on the international capital markets and allow them to manage their debts more effectively. The injection of capital investment in these countries would stimulate growth with benefits for both investors and capital recipients.

After the 1973-74 OPEC oil price increases and the accumulation of capital-surplus funds by some oil-producing countries, a debate was opened regarding the ways and means to invest these surpluses most productively. The debate seemed settled in favor of concentrated investments in the national economies, as a first priority, and in the industrialized countries as a second alternative. While concentrated investment in the national economies continues to command faithful observance, there are reasons to question the soundness of the second alternative, in view of the accumulated experiences of the 1970s. Political and economic developments in the last few years have called for reopening the debate on appropriate strategies for the investment capital surplus.

This chapter will review some of the arguments advanced during the first round of the debate and evaluate them in light of the experiences of the 1970s. We shall discuss the political, economic, and legal constraints evolved in industrialized countries against OPEC's capital-surplus investments; present the case in favor of increased investment in developing countries; and finally, we shall provide a sketchy profile of Latin America as a dynamic region where increased capital-surplus investments could be beneficial for both the capital-surplus oil exporters and Latin American countries.

Investment Strategies of Capital Surplus

It is difficult to estimate the amount of capital-surplus oil funds with any accuracy. Measured by the current account surpluses of Saudi Arabia, Kuwait, Libya, Iraq, Qatar, and the United Arab Emirates

(UAE) between 1973 and 1980, capital-surplus oil funds are estimated at some $350 billion. But they could be twice that level.[8] Others estimate they will reach $500 billion by 1982.[9] "Secrecy theorists" contend that the surpluses are much larger, but their figures are known only to the capital-surplus countries and some Western governments, particularly the United States.[10]

Capital surplus was the result of overproduction of oil to meet the world demand. Some producers found it necessary to produce oil above their financial need because of their own stake in the heart of the world economy.[11]

If the obligation to maintain current levels of oil production —and consequently the accumulation of large capital surpluses—is inescapable, they must find ways to protect their surpluses against inflation and currency devaluation. At least three strategies were advanced in the 1970s as to how these surplus funds should be invested: the first was articulated by Arab economists; the second by the banking community; and the third by international development institutions and Western liberals.

Arab economists placed priority on investment in the Arab world. They argued that while some Arab oil producers have limited absorptive capacity, that of the Arab world as a whole is almost limitless.[12] They maintained that oil revenues are not income on capital, but rather they themselves are the capital because they are paid in compensation for the loss of a finite natural resource.[13] Therefore, the surpluses should be invested where the loss takes place, broadly defined to include Arab non–oil-producing countries as well. These economists shared the view that investment in the Arab world is safer and provides higher return and less risk in the long run considering inflation.[14] Some argued that even the use of the term *surplus* is inaccurate, since there is no surplus as far as the development of the Arab world is concerned.[15] For example, the cost of a comprehensive educational program in the Arab world was estimated to be about $25 billion a year. The minimum cost of a highway network linking the Arab countries was put at about $100 billion, and the minimum cost of medical facilities for the Arab world was put at about $35 billion.[16] Others argued for the use of surplus revenues to secure "special benefits," such as technological transfer, and to foster Arab national interests.[17]

These views were received with some skepticism by other Arab economists. For example, Abdlatif Y. al-Hamad argued that the absorptive capacity of the Arab world as a whole is limited in the short run.[18] After reviewing all possibilities for investment in the Arab world and considering its limited absorptive capacity in the short run, he concluded that "within the confines of the Arab world, and given certain assumptions concerning the ceiling that can be reached by inter-Arab finance of real investments, no solution to the recycling problem can occur through the exchange of already existing real assets, or through the exchange of financial investments or monetary liability between different Arab markets."[19]

The second view was articulated by both Arab and Western bankers and was based on commercial considerations. Arab bankers stressed that surplus funds must be invested wherever the return on investment was highest. Salim Hoss offered two arguments for this view: first, oil is a depletive asset and therefore investment should be considered a substitute resource equal in value to the oil; and second, investment should provide returns immune from the attrition of currency devaluations (or depreciation). He put forth two investment strategies: (1) a preference for short-term investments which would allow capital-exporting countries a minimum leeway of maneuverability; and (2) direct investments in real estate and industrial equities in the developed world.[20] Other Arab advocates of the same view pointed out the inevitability of concentrating investment in the European and U.S. markets because only these markets have the breadth and depth to accommodate such surpluses.[21]

G.A. Costanzo presented the perspective of the Western banking community. He maintained that the oil producers "lack sufficient manpower to execute the kinds of managerial, technical and productive functions essential to complete their elaborate domestic development plans."[22] Consequently, surplus funds should be channeled to where they can be managed efficiently—the industrialized world.

The third view was articulated by an assortment of Western liberals and development institutions concerned with the stability of the international economic order and development in the Third World. Guy Erb represented this view in his work on financing international development. He indicated that the oil price increases of 1973–74 caused imbalances in the financial obligations of all nations of the world. They created "petrodollar crisis [which] disrupted established patterns of international relations . . . [and] added to the woes of industrialized and developing nations."[23] To achieve a stable international economic order a recycling strategy was needed to redistribute the funds among all states affected by the oil price increases. He advised the U.S. government to encourage a "cooperation approach," since without it the United States would see piecemeal erosion of its influence within the very multilateral systems it helped create. A recycling strategy was imperative because "the interrelationships between the United States and [other] nations made it impossible to shield the U.S. economy entirely from the deflationary impact of declines in foreign economic activity.'' The impact of events in other industrial countries was particularly important for the United States, but a widespread economic recession in Africa, Asia, and Latin America could also have significant repercussions on its economy. The failure of allocating financial resources which enable individual nations to meet their oil-import requirements may lead to the curtailment of their nonoil imports.[24]

The debate on investment strategies was resolved in a sharing formula that satisfied the three arguments, but left the developing countries in a least favorable position as their indebtedness soared in the 1970s. Oil-exporting countries sought to increase their expenditures for development in what seems to be a race with inflation which has constantly affected the value of their oil revenues. They have also extended generous economic assistance to other developing countries, either on a bilateral basis or through multilateral financing institutions.[25] But most capital surplus has been invested in the Western banking system, in equity, real estate, and similar types of investment. Increasingly these investments are facing economic, political, and legal constraints in industrialized countries. A new round of debate is timely for increasing investments in developing countries directly by the capital-surplus oil exporters.

Constraints on Investment

The experiences of the 1970s have shown that investment in industrialized countries could face serious economic risks. These are of two types: one is the constant depreciation of the value of the surpluses due to inflation, currency devaluation, etc., and the other is the economic cost of increased dependency. The first type of risk was discussed briefly above and bears on the prospects of growth in the Western economies that have been plagued by stagflation and low productivity. In the 1970s capital surpluses suffered because of high rates of inflation and currency devaluation. Especially affected were portfolio investments in dollar securities and bank deposits which experienced a decline in value, sometimes with negative returns.[26]

The second and probably more important risk is related to the economic cost of dependency on industrialized countries. The continuing controversy between industrialized and developing countries, particularly between the former and OPEC, regarding energy, trade relations, and transfer of technology will remain sources of friction beyond the stage of the development of alternative sources of energy. Apart from its use as a source of energy, oil is an essential component of modern technology, as in petrochemicals and food production. By concentrating their investments in the advanced countries, the surplus fund countries increase the risks inherent in such a strategy in time of conflict of interests. Industrialized countries could inflict losses on the financial assets of the surplus fund countries by manipulating the market price of such assets as one means of adjusting to the higher prices of oil. That could be accomplished by devaluing their currency, raising the price of their commodities, or any combination thereof.

Political constraints on capital surplus funds were best revealed in the 1970s in the action taken by the U.S. government to freeze Iranian assets in U.S. banks and their branches overseas.[27] Given the tenuous state of affairs between the United States and some Arab oil-producing countries, the possibility of the United States freezing their assets cannot be discounted as a political risk. The concentration of capital-surplus investment in the industrialized countries makes capital-surplus countries susceptible to pressure and compromise in their bargaining position regarding issues such as energy, trade, and technology transfer. This situation is in contrast to the commonly accepted notion of international interdependence because it tends to keep the gap between industrialized and developing countries.

Legal constraints against OPEC surplus investments in the industrialized countries developed gradually in a variety of legislation and recommendations. Only a few examples will be provided here to demonstrate the general negative orientation—and tone—predominant in the industrialized countries, particularly against Arab investments.

In the United States, proposals were advanced in the mid-1970s to limit the ceiling of foreign investment in certain industries and prohibit them altogether in others.[28] The U.S. Congress passed the Foreign Investment Study Act on October 26, 1974, to investigate and review all aspects of foreign investments in the United States. The major objective of this legislation was to monitor the transfer of equity ownership of U.S. corporations to the hands of foreigners. Of particular concern to the Congress was possible use of surplus funds for the purchase of substantial or controlling shares of major U.S. industrial and financial corporations. Since then the U.S. government and Congress have produced a multiplicity of laws and regulations that negatively affect Arab investments and trade.[29] Surplus funds have been restricted to marginal sectors such as government bonds and other "harmless" enterprises like real estate developments.[30]

In Great Britain, a negative feeling also developed against the investment of surplus oil funds, even at a time when its economy depended on them.[31] In the mid-1970s, the British press made an issue of

Kuwait's offer to buy a real estate company in the amount of 107 million pounds. There was no objection made to Kuwait as a shareholder in British companies, but, as one commentator put it, "total ownership is, of course, another matter."[32] Suggestions were made to the British government to nationalize those economic sectors attractive to oil producers in order to protect them against investment takeover.[33]

West Germany followed the same pattern. This was championed by Franz Ulrich, chairman of both the Deutsche Bank and Mannesmann, the leading steel and machine company. His objective was to "counter potential take-overs of crucial industrial concerns by undesirable foreign investors."[34] In support of this position, the Ministry of Economics published a list of 500 companies in which foreign participation "would not be desirable."[35]

In spite of these restrictions, investments have been concentrated in the advanced countries, a practice that can be questioned as a viable strategy. It leads to narrow trade relations of excess fund countries and results in stronger dependency on industrialized countries. Financial dealings with these countries will naturally lead to broader trade relations with them at the expense of other countries, which may be more profitable to the surplus fund countries. Standardized commodities and food products, for example, can be obtained cheaper from many sources in the Third World, particularly from countries that stress export promotion as a strategy for development, such as Brazil, South Korea, Taiwan, and Mexico. But the lack of direct financial dealings with these countries operates against surplus fund countries capitalizing on the economic benefits available to them.

Investment in the Third World

The foregoing arguments dealt with the economic, political, and legal constraints associated with the concentration of investment in the industrialized countries. Some capital-surplus oil producers have come to recognize that industrialized countries are not yet prepared, politically and/or psychologically, to accept non-Western investment, and have therefore decided to reduce their investments, particularly in the United States.[36] Proposals have been advanced to explore investment opportunities somewhere else in the Arab world and in other developing countries.

Regarding investment in the Arab world, the constraint of absorptive capacity was mentioned earlier in this chapter. Until more favorable economic and political conditions prevail in the Arab world, investments are unlikely to reach their potential level. Where investments are needed most, conditions favorable to such investments are still lacking. These conditions are: availability of efficient communication systems (telephone, mail, road, railways, etc.); economic development plans and legal systems that safeguard the equity position of their investments. Added to these factors is investors' fear of political instability, whether related to the Arab/Israeli conflict or to internal problems. In the long run, favorable conditions could be developed and investments in the Arab world would be expected to expand.[37]

It has been argued that growing proportions of Arab surplus funds will inevitably find their way to other developing countries where rates of return could be higher. Some have argued for increased investment in these countries under a new division of labor and production.[38] Others have argued that a sense of commitment rather than purely economic considerations must prevail. Iraq, for example, has suggested that surplus funds should be invested either in the Arab world or in other developing countries as a principle of solidarity and because this would create economic cohesion among them.[39] Similarly, Kuwait has stressed the need for cooperation with developing countries based on "enlightened self-interest."[40]

Solidarity among developing countries must also be an important consideration for surplus fund countries in their choice of investment strategies. For example, in solidarity with OPEC, developing countries chose not to oppose its oil price increases because they perceived OPEC's action as one round in the battle against exploitation which would ultimately benefit them all.[41] To their consternation, they discovered that they had to pay substantially higher prices for imported oil, which almost wrecked their economies. OPEC countries came to their help, but the provisional nature of their aid and loans did not ease much of their overburdened balance-of-payments deficits, particularly after the second oil price increases in 1979-80. Developing countries need more investment capital, and this has not been forthcoming. Consequently, a crack in the solidarity principle seems to be growing. This threatens to generate clashes of interest between OPEC and other developing countries. Jealousy alone could be a potentially destructive force if put to work against OPEC.[42] Once this point of divisiveness is reached, the system of solidarity could break down and OPEC members would suffer the consequences.

Capital-surplus countries would also be advised to recognize that true interdependence is a system of balanced economic relations with all other countries of the world, and that reliance on industrialized countries to the exclusion of developing ones will not benefit them in the long run.[43] Since reluctance to invest in developing countries reflects negative perceptions of them as a viable alternative to investment in industrialized countries, some discussion will be devoted to dispel these negative perceptions. Most arguments against investment in developing countries center around two issues: first, the lack of knowledge, expertise, communication systems, investment opportunities; and second, political instability.

Reservations generated by the first set of arguments can be eliminated or tempered after the political decision is made to explore investment opportunities in developing countries. The institutions and expertise necessary for the identification and implementation of investment projects can be developed by the surplus fund countries to channel investment capital to the developing world. The surplus fund countries can acquire this knowledge faster than Westerners, simply because they are familiar with the conditions of underdevelopment.

The question of inadequacy of communication systems, transport lines, etc., is also surmountable. Communication and trade routes between developing regions existed before the advent of colonialism. One of the consequences of the Industrial Revolution was the domination of established territorial and sea routes by the Western metropolis, which became the center of all communication and commerce. The reestablishment of these routes by the newly independent and sovereign countries is inseparable from the whole process of decolonialization. Fortunately, this task is greatly facilitated today by the advances in communication and transport technology. Channeling surplus funds to developing countries will serve to realign the trade routes and lines of communication, as well as redistribute knowledge and expertise. A precondition to such a development is the emergence of a political will on the part of the surplus fund countries to invest in the developing world.

A more serious argument is that related to instability. There is certainly a number of cases of expropriations in developing countries to warrant this uneasiness. But the tendency to generalize often corresponds with imprecision. A few points can be made in this regard:

1. The perception of developing countries' instability is created by the advanced countries simply because they suffered most from expropriation. The latter occurred mostly during the era of colonialism and represented to the newly independent countries the remnants of colonial rule. Most of these interests were exploitative in nature and nationalization was overdue. The history of the oil industry in Middle East, or the copper industry in Chile, for example, are cases in point. To my knowledge there are no cases of expropriation of investments of developing countries in other developing countries.

2. The claim of instability of developing countries serves to discourage the surplus fund countries from initiating direct contact with them. Certainly Western bankers would be adversely affected by such direct contacts, since it is mainly from Western financial markets that developing countries obtain most of their loans. There is no evidence to suggest that the movement of capital from these markets to developing countries has slowed down in the last decade. On the contrary, capital movement from the Western financial markets to the developing countries has expanded from $16 billion in 1971 to $209 billion in 1981.[44] The interest costs of these loans to developing countries have been above the prime leading rates and have resulted in substantial windfall profits to Western banks.

3. Developing countries are mindful of their previous experiences with multinational corporations and are careful that exploitation will not recur. Such sensitivity has been interpreted as cause for potential instability. Understandably, developing countries want to reduce the chances of exploitation by imposing certain limitations on foreign investment. In spite of that, the most stringent restrictions on foreign investments are found in the advanced rather than the developing countries. The latter have accepted the concept of joint venture and provided tax exemptions and capital repatriation provisions to foreign investors.

Investment in Latin America

Investment in Latin American countries offers advantages that may not be present in industrialized countries and are certainly not available in at least some developing countries. Latin America is a wide expanse of territories, with a variety of climates, natural resources, and opportunities. The continent's Spanish and Portuguese populations are endowed with a great deal of imagination, ambition, and talent. Latin America also provides a variety of political and economic systems, yet it constitutes a world by itself in terms of culture and civilization. Investors in Latin America have a wide choice of opportunities and are disposed to shift their investments from one part of the continent to another. Of the twenty-nine countries in Central and South America some, such as Brazil, Mexico, and Argentina, are considered newly industrialized, while others, such as the small republics in the Caribbean, are considered low- or middle-income countries. The more developed countries present the characteristics of both the developed and developing countries, with their advantages and handicaps. Infrastructures such as roads, communication systems, electricity, etc., are laid down and progressively expanded from the urban centers to the rural peripheries. Investors move into a climate already explored and shaped by American, European, and

Japanese investors. Incentives for foreign investments are specified, and restrictions and regulations are clearly outlined. The expectation of profits is well established, and the right to profit repatriation is recognized. Change of government, whether by democratic means or military juntas, rarely affects this investment climate. This stability is responsible for the continued inflow of capital to Latin America during the last three decades.

Industrialization in Latin American countries have resulted in the development of a highly qualified labor force to fill professional, managerial, and technical positions. These countries have also developed sophisticated banking systems and advanced research and marketing facilities. These banking systems operate strictly under the guidance of central banks, a protection to foreign investors not often provided in some industrialized countries. In addition, Latin American countries provide large markets for industrial products. Since the rate of consumerism is normally considered an index of prosperity, Latin Americans have developed their consumer habits and have worked hard to maintain them. This orientation has assured foreign investors a steady growth of their investments.

The surplus fund countries could find in Latin America additional advantages if they shifted their investment strategies from short-term financial payoffs to long-term profits, both economic and political. In their effort to industrialize, they could turn to Latin American countries for help, particularly to the newly industrialized countries. By establishing joint ventures they would be better equipped to absorb smoothly the process of technology transfer without facing the technological onslaught they have been subjected to in the last decade.

Most surplus fund countries are dependent on industrialized countries for food. In times of crisis such dependence could be detrimental to their interests. It is imperative that they develop alternative sources of food for the future. The surplus fund countries could invest in agriculture in Latin America and establish their own sources of food. The potential of Latin American agricultural resources, whether for food such as wheat or for industry such as wood and paper, is most important in a world increasingly characterized by commodity shortages and rising prices.

More could be said about the advantages the surplus fund countries could derive from investing in developing countries generally and in Latin America particularly. In the final analysis this option will depend on how much talent, foresight, and courage they can muster and display in coming years. In the words of Robert McNamara, former president of the World Bank, "the parable of the talent is about financial power—and it illuminates the great truth that all power is given us to be used, not to be wrapped in a napkin against risk."[45]

Notes

1. *World Development Report, 1981* (Washington, D.C.: World Bank, August 1981), p. 8.
2. These countries comprise Iraq, Kuwait, Libya, Saudi Arabia, Qatar, and the United Arab Emirates. Ibid., p. viii.
3. See Chandra S. Hardy, "Adjustment to Global Payments Imbalances: A Tripartite Solution," Working Paper no. 5, Overseas Development Council, Washington, D.C., September 1981, pp. 18-19.
4. W. Arthur Lewis, "The Slowing Down of the Engine of Growth," *American Economic Review* 70 (September 1980):555-64.
5. The magnitude of the developing countries' indebtedness problem is the subject of an ever-widening literature. An investigation of this problem and relation to the oil capital-surplus funds is provided by Fehmy Saddy, "OPEC Capital-Surplus Funds and Third World Indebtedness: The 'Recycling' Strategy Considered," *Third World Quarterly* 4 (October 1982): 736-57.
6. Organization for Economic Cooperation and Development, Development Cooperation Directorats, "External Debt Statistics for Developing Countries: Latest Trends," Document DCD 181.33, September 22, 1981.
7. Ralph C. Bryant, "Notes on the Analysis of Capital Flows to Developing Nations and the 'Recycling' Problem," World Bank Staff Working Paper no. 476, Washington, D.C., August 1981, p. 58.
8. Hardy, p. 18.
9. "Morgan Guarantee Warns on Massive OPEC Revenue," *International Herald Tribune*, December 10, 1979, p. 1.
10. "Saudi-American Finances—That Secret Agreement: Final Confirmation and Assessment of Its Long-Term Importance," *International Currency Review* 12 (1980):7-24.
11. There are other reasons for the overproduction of oil which are political and economic. For example, the ability of Saudi Arabia to increase its production in 1979 alleviated the shortage in the world oil market that developed after the Iranian Revolution and prevented other OPEC members from raising the price of their oil. This capability is translated into economic power. In addition, Saudi Arabia fears that substantial increases of oil prices would accelerate the process of developing alternative sources of energy by the industrialized countries and ultimately result in depressing oil prices.
12. Nicholas Sarkis defended this view. *Lisan Al-Hal*, Beirut, September 14, 1974, p. 4 (in Arabic).
13. Muhammad Atallah articulated this view, but in the context of making the argument for surplus investment in developed countries. *Lisan Al-Hal*, Beirut, September 29, 1974 (in Arabic).
14. This view was shared by the participants in a seminar on the subject by the Forum of Development Studies in Beirut. *Lisan Al-Hal*, Beirut, November 29, 1975, p. 2 (in Arabic).
15. Sarkis, p. 4.
16. These views were expressed at a conference organized by the *Financial Times* in Beirut on September 22-23, 1974, under the rubric "The Middle East in World Finance." *Middle East Economic Digest*, September 27, 1974, p. 1140.

17. Omar Kassem, "The Attitude of the Oil States to Recycling and the U.S.," *Euromoney*, March 1975, p. 14.
18. "Surplus Oil Funds and the Arab Capital Market," *Euromoney*, February, 1975, pp. 17-22.
19. Ibid., p. 20.
20. "Developing Long-Term Channels for Arab Oil Money," *Euromoney*, October 1974, pp. 75-77.
21. Hikmat Sh. Nashashibi, "Other Ways to Recycle Oil Surplus," *Euromoney*, August 1974, p. 52.
22. "Oil Lands Can't Buy Up U.S. Industry," *New York Times*, June 1, 1975, p. 14.
23. "Petrodollars and Multilateral Development Financing," in *The U.S. and World Development: Agenda for Action, 1975*, ed. James W. Howe (New York: Praeger, 1975), p. 106.
24. Ibid., p. 107.
25. In spite of the increased indebtedness of LDCs, aid from developed countries as a percentage of their GNPs declined from 0.30 percent in 1974 to 0.22 percent in 1977. This was way below the recommended target of 0.7 percent for the UN Second Development Decade. By comparison, OPEC members committed 8.2 percent of their GNPs in aid in 1974, the first year after the oil price increases. Organization for Economic Cooperation and Development, Development Assistance Directorate, *Flow of Resources from OPEC Members to Developing Countries*, Document no. DD 403, December 6, 1975, table 2, p. 8. The estimated figures of Official Development Assistance of OECD countries in 1980 is $26.6 billion, or 0.37 percent of their GNPs; for OAPEC countries they are $6.80 billion, or 2.34 percent. *World Development Report, 1981*, table 16, "Official Development Assistance from OECD and OPEC Members," pp. 164-65. See also "Arab Institutions for Development Aid Have Rapidly Expanded Their Activities," *IMF Survey*, February 5, 1969, p. 37; "Arab Monetary Fund Loan Operations Begin with Payments Assistance for Five Members," *IMF Survey*, August 20, 1979, pp. 249-50.
26. Jahangir Amuzegar, "OPEC and the Dollar Dilemma," *Foreign Affairs* 56 (1978):740-50.
27. The effect of the freeze was not confined to the action of the U.S. government of Iran, its instrumentalities, controlled utilities, and the Central Bank of Iran, as the Presidential Order specified. Currently thousands of litigations are being pursued by U.S. companies against Iranian citizens and companies involving attachment of their properties.
28. See Gregory E. Andrews, "An Evaluation of the Need for Further Statutory Control on Foreign Direct Investment in the United States," *Vanderbilt Journal of International Law* 8 (1974):147-87; John Young, "The Acquisition of United States Businesses by Foreign Investors," *Business Lawyer* 30 (1974):111-28; Philip T. Kaplan, "Buying a U.S. Company," *Bulletin of International Financial Documentation* 29 (1971): 3-18; "New Invasions by Oil Money," *U.S. News and World Report*, March 3, 1975, pp. 21-23; "Is There Any Way to Beat the Arabs at Their Money Game," *U.S. News and World Report*, December 16, 1974, pp. 60-61.
29. See Public Law no. 95-52, title II, 91 stat. 235, Export Administration

Amendments (1977), amending 50 U.S.C. §2401 et seq. (1970); Henry J. Steiner, "International Boycotts and Domestic Order: American Involvement in the Arab–Israeli Conflict," *Texas Law Review* 54 (1976): 1355–1410; "U.S. Regulation of Direct Foreign Investment: Current Developments and the Congressional Response," *Virginia Journal of International Law* 15 (1975):611-47.

30.   Even this "harmless" type of investment stirred up opposition in the United States. See Priscilla S. Maya, "Atlantic Squabbles: Kuwait's Resort Off Coast of Carolina Proceeds amid Wild Rumors, Stiff Opposition," *Wall Street Journal*, February 26, 1975, p. 38.

31.   Great Britain was able to overcome its strenuous economic crisis of 1973–74 due to the fact that 26 percent of all payments for oil to Saudi Arabia and all payments to Kuwait and the United Arab Emirates were kept in sterling in British banks. Fouad Abi-Saleh, "Putting Oil Revenues in Their Proper Context," *Euromoney*, October 1974, p. 88.

32.   Christopher Fildes, "Kuwait: What That $107 M. Bid Portends," *Euromoney*, October 1974, p. 99.

33.   *Lisan Al-Hal*, Beirut, September 17, 1974 (in Arabic).

34.   "Bonn Acts to Curb Oil Nation Zest for European Investments," *Christian Science Monitor*, May 28, 1975, p. 21.

35.   The report further proposed that all foreign capital investments that exceed 10 percent of a company whose turnover exceeds 100 million marks, or investments that surpass 100 million marks are subject to prior notification to the Ministry of Economics. Ibid.

36.   "OPEC Countries Reduce Deposits in U.S. Banks," *New York Times*, January 19, 1982, p. D1.

37.   Fouad Abi-Saleh, p. 85.

38.   Anthony Asseily, "Hustling the East into Recycling Its Funds," *Euromoney*, July 1974, p. 22.

39.   Reported in *Lisan Al-Hal*, Beirut, October 3, 1974 (in Arabic).

40.   "Hamad Calls for Joint Effort to Face Food Crisis," *Middle East Economic Digest*, September 2, 1974, p. 1090.

41.   Another consideration was that they hoped to follow in OPEC's footsteps by forming cartels of their own. They discovered that they could not control the prices of their products because the need for them was not as pressing as that for oil.

42.   Survey research conducted in some developing countries revealed a negative image of OPEC. See Fehmy Saddy, "OPEC, the Arabs, and the Less Developed Countries," *Journal of Arab Politics* 1 (April 1982).

43.   See Fehmy Saddy,' "A World Economic Order: The Limits of Accommodation," *International Journal* 34 (Winter 1979):16-38.

44.   OECD, "External Debt Statistics."

45.   *One Hundred Countries, Two Billion People: The Dimensions of Development* (New York: Praeger, 1973), p. 20.

8
Oil-Exporting Countries' Investment Portfolio: Diversification toward Latin America

Carlos Massad

The oil-exporting countries are extracting wealth from the ground to secure a future stream of income. Instead of investing by leaving oil underground, they are extracting enough oil to maintain a given level of consumption and make other investments. Placement of funds in the monetary and financial markets as well as acquisition of real assets are part and parcel of this policy. Yields in different financial markets, including allowances for exchange rate movements and risks tend rapidly to attain equality, since financial resources can move easily from one market to another. The composition of a given portfolio of financial investments will be very influenced by the investor's possibility of predicting, better than the market, future variations of exchange and interest rates.

This is not so where the acquisition of real assets is concerned. Rates of return on investments in real assets differ among countries tending to equality with extremely long delays, while the variability of those returns also differ from country to country. Commodities, labor, technology, and capital goods do not move with the same ease as financial resources, and natural elements such as climate, land quality, altitude, etc., are extremely expensive to reproduce in a different environment. The composition of an investment portfolio in real assets is influenced by a large number of factors, from religious and cultural considerations to economic and security factors. This is not necessarily so in the case of financial investments, since the cost of changing the portfolio composition in such a case is not substantial. The cost of changing the composition of a real assets investment portfolio is usually higher, so that such composition will be more influenced by long-run considerations.

The purpose of this chapter is to explore the economic advantages for Arab oil-exporting countries to internationally diversify their real assets investment portfolio by giving higher importance to investments in Latin America. The first part of the chapter examines the use of foreign savings in Latin American development and the main factors that have tended to increase the area's reliance on resources from abroad and hence Latin American demand for foreign savings. The second part explores the possibility of international diversification of investments of Arab oil-exporting countries and the economic advantages of increasing the share of their investments in Latin America. It also examines briefly other areas of financial cooperation and some possible institutional channels to facilitate investment diversification of the investing countries.

Domestic and Foreign Savings in Latin America

Past and Present Trends

The non–oil-exporting countries of Latin America have been traditionally net users of foreign savings. Their balance of payments' current accounts have been persistently in deficit, which reached a yearly average for the group of around $2 billion in 1965-70. This was a complement to domestic savings and ensured investment levels high enough to contribute to an economic growth rate of 6 percent as an average for the period, and slightly lower than that for the decade of the 1960s. During this period, domestic savings were used to finance 85 percent of gross domestic fixed investment, while deficit in the balance of payments' current account covered the rest.

The balance-of-payments disequilibrium referred to above, which represented about 16 percent of total exports of goods and services, did not create generalized balance-of-payments problems. Exports were growing rapidly, while the financing of the current imbalance came from direct foreign investment, borrowing from official and private sources in approximately equal shares. Since borrowing from official sources usually involves medium- or long-term debt, the form taken by foreign financing did not create an excessive burden in any particular future period and the foreign debt profile of the region showed an adequate distribution of debt repayments through time.

The second half of the 1960s and the early 1970s witnessed an impressive expansion of foreign trade by non–oil-exporting countries in Latin America. Total exports grew at an annual average rate of almost 17 percent through agressive efforts in most countries to gradually open their economies and expand exports at the subregional, regional, and world levels. Such efforts included the application in some inflation-ridden countries of smaller and frequent adjustments in the nominal exchange rate to avoid sharp fluctuations in the real rate. Multiple exchange rate practices were substantially eliminated in most countries and a general environment of openness in trade substituted the highly protectionist trends prevailing in the previous decade. Sustained expansion of the world economy with relative price stability in the latter part of the 1950s and through the 1960s provided the appropriate framework for outward growth of most Latin American countries.

Through this period, increasing demand for foreign reserves in Europe and Japan provided a counterpart to persistent deficits in the U.S. balance of payments. The monetary system of Western countries worked smoothly and international money and capital markets reappeared after the collapse that followed the Great Depression of the thirties. As their external economic relations expanded, the larger countries in Latin America—and some of the smaller ones—found increasing access to private foreign banks as sources of credit. Latin American trade expansion helped in this direction, but the ground was set by the rapid growth of European currency markets (see Tables 8.1 and 8.2).

TABLE 8.1
Non–Oil-Exporting Developing Countries of Latin America:[1]
Current Account Financing ($ billions)

	Annual Average		1977	1978	1979
	1966-1970	1974-1976			
Current Account deficit 2/	-2.0	-13.6	-7.9	-10.5	-18.0
Variation of reserve assets	0.4	0.7	3.9	7.6	5.5
Requirements	2.4	14.3	11.8	18.1	23.5
Net External financing	2.5	13.6	12.7	16.3	24.4
Direct investment	0.7	2.1	2.3	3.0	3.0
Grants	0.1	0.1	0.2	0.2	0.2
Net Borrowing	1.7	11.4	10.2	13.1	21.2
Official sources	0.9	2.0	2.2	2.9	3.0
Multilateral	0.4	0.9	1.2	1.5	1.5
Bilateral	0.5	1.1	1.0	1.4	1.5
Private sources	0.8	9.5	8.0	10.2	18.2
Suppliers credits	0.4	0.5	1.2	2.2	1.0
Private banks	0.3	8.0	4.7	5.8	18.0
Other sources and errors	0.4	1.0	2.1	2.2	-0.8

1. Includes Mexico and Peru.
2. Net total balance on goods and services, and private transfers.

Sources: ECLA, "Balance of Payments," on the Basis of data published by *International Monetary Fund* (IMF), September 1981; IDB, "External public debt of the Latin American Countries," (Washington, D.C. July 1981); BIS, "Animal Reports" and "Supplements"; and ECLA estimates.

TABLE 8.2
Non–Oil-Exporting Countries in Latin America: Foreign and
Domestic Financing of Gross Domestic Fixed Investment (%) [1]

	1960–1961	1969–1970	1974–1975	1978–1979
Domestic savings	85.8	91.6	78.1	84.9
Current account deficit	14.2	8.4	21.9	15.1
	100.0	100.0	100.0	100.0

1. Calculated by converting national currencies to dollars, through applying conversion factors published in IMF, *International Financial Statistics,* various issues.

Source: ECLA, "Balance of Payments" and "National Accounts," on the basis of data provided by the IMF and reporting countries, September 1981.

In the early 1980s, the continued deficit in the U.S. balance of payments together with the growth of European currency markets gave rise to the expectation that some European currencies would be revalued against the dollar. Such expectation produced sizable capital movements which countries were unable to control. Economic circumstances thus compelled important industrial countries to float their currencies, marking the beginning of a new state of adjustment in the world economy. Inflationary tendencies already present in the late 1960s became more evident and proved more stubborn than in the past, so that antiinflationary policy resulted more in a weakening of the growth rate of the world economy than in a substantial alleviation of rapidly increasing prices.

Oil price increases at the end of 1973, a consequence of such trends, accentuated them and contributed to a modification of the traditional structure of world balance of payments. The current account deficit of non–oil-exporting countries in Latin America, which had already doubled to about $4 billion in the early 1970s, increased substantially to an average of $13 billion in 1974-79. Industrial countries, which traditionally registered a current account surplus, showed a substantial deficit in 1974, which gave additional stimulus to the application of restrictive economic policies.

As a consequence of this situation the increase in the external gap of non–oil-exporting countries in Latin America was accompanied by a substantial reduction in the relative importance of direct foreign investment and borrowing from official sources, while borrowing from commercial banks increased markedly to fill the gap. Borrowing from commercial banks abroad in the second half of the 1970s was 32 times larger than the yearly average of the second half of the 1960s. At the same time, loan terms deteriorated: the concessionality factor decreased by almost 73 percent in 1969–79 (see Table 8.3). The increased current account imbalance induced non–oil-exporting Latin American countries both to look for additional financing and to adopt adjustment policies to avoid excessive sacrifice in terms of their growth rate.

TABLE 8.3
DAC Member Countries and Multilateral Agencies:[a] Geographic Distribution of Net Financial Flows Transfer to Non–Oil-Exporting Developing Countries ($ billions)

	1969			1975			1979		
	Total	Concessional	2/1	Total	Concessional	2/1	Total	Concessional	2/1
Latin America	2.64	0.81	30.5	7.19	1.07	14.9	18.62	1.55	8.3
Africa [b]	2.08	1.35	64.8	6.51	3.91	60.0	16.60	8.70	52.4
Asia [c]	3.86	2.49	64.5	6.57	3.94	60.0	17.74	9.28	52.3
Europe [d]	1.41	0.31	22.3	3.57	0.63	17.7	8.33	1.99	23.9
Other	0.28	0.22	80.7	0.68	0.61	90.7	1.01	0.88	87.1

[a] Multilateral agencies with concessional component in their lending of less than 25% are not included.
[b] Excludes Gabon, Nigeria, and Algeria.
[c] Excludes Middle East, Israel, and Indonesia.
[d] Includes Portugal, Cyprus, Gilbraltar, Greece, Malta, Spain, Turkey, Yugoslavia, and Israel.

Sources: OECD, "Geographical distribution of financial flows to developing countries 1969-1975" (Paris 1977); and OECD, Development Cooperation Review (1980).

The general outcome of these policies is one of success. The current account deficit increased again after 1978, but economic growth rates, even though lower than early in the decade, were higher than those registered in other areas of the world. The region also kept high investment rates to ensure a sustained growth in the future. Investment rates in 1975–76 were higher than in any year since 1966. The policy mix of adjustment and financing in Latin America resulted in a reduction in the external imbalance without sacrificing either investment rates or future growth rates. ECLA data show that investment rates over gross domestic product, which were 17.6 percent in 1966, grew steadily to an average of 21.7 percent in 1975–80.

Adjustment, Financing, or Both: The Picture of the Near Future

The level of current account external imbalance of recent years will probably be lower in the future. Oil-exporting countries' imports are expected to continue growing rapidly. Policies in industrial countries will probably be more successful than they have been in diminishing substantial imbalances among them, so that the sum total of surpluses in the world economy should decrease, with a corresponding decrease in deficits.

It is unlikely that imbalance figures will go back in the near future to the magnitudes registered before 1974. Between 1967 and 1973, the sum total of current account deficits of IMF member countries reached an annual average of $13 billion, which jumped to an average of over $82 billion in 1973–80. If this figure were to decrease continuously at a rate of $10 billion per year, a rate high enough to be rather improbable, it would take six to seven years for the annual figure to return to the 1967–73 average. Most probably, the time required would be even longer.

As a byproduct of this general picture, non–oil-exporting developing countries, including those of Latin America, will register a sustained deficit in their current account balance of payments for a relatively long time. If deficit countries as a whole made efforts to eliminate the deficit, they would only succeed in transferring it elsewhere. Insofar as there remain sizable surpluses in the world, they must have a counterpart in the form of deficits. The only alternative would be a substantial reduction in world income, an option rejected by all concerned.

Latin American non–oil-exporting countries—and maybe some oil-exporting ones—will register a deficit in their current account balance of payments and will continue to demand foreign savings, under one form or another, for some time to come. This would not be so, or at least not in the same magnitude, if these countries were to reduce their income and investment level and/or if they were in a position to accept a substantial reduction in their external reserves. Latin American countries are making efforts to reduce their external disequilibrium to more manageable proportions, and the question is whether the world economy is interested in providing foreign savings to prevent *excessive* adjustment policies in Latin America. I think the answer to this question must be positive.

Even though some countries of the region have accumulated external reserves which are substantial in absolute magnitude, they are not higher as a proportion of imports than they were in 1951–55, also a period of high reserves by historical standards (see Table 8.4). The fact that there is easier access to short-term financing in the European currency markets acts toward reducing the amount of reserves needed; but terms of trade have shown a volatility in the 1970s that justifies additional prudence in reserve management.

TABLE 8.4
Non–Oil-Exporting Developing Countries of Latin America:
Reserves as a Proportion of Imports—
Selected Countries and Periods (%)

Country	1951–55	1956–60	1961–65	1966–70	1971–73	1974–80
Argentina	40.0	24.2	15.7	34.9	29.4	64.1
Bolivia	19.9	5.7	12.6	20.7	22.9	22.1
Brazil	29.7	27.7	23.1	23.1	71.3	41.1
Chile	16.8	17.0	12.8	25.2	13.3	35.1
Colombia	30.7	27.9	14.7	16.9	26.7	72.6
Ecuador	37.3	24.2	27.4	24.6	34.6	32.3
Guatemala	45.8	37.0	29.0	23.2	34.4	37.5
Mexico	29.7	33.5	29.5	24.2	27.8	17.7
Uruguay	112.2	84.7	86.7	74.0	65.8	65.6

Sources: IMF, *International Financial Statistics* (May 1978); ECLA, "Balance of Payments," on the basis of data published by the IMF, September 1981.

Reductions in income and investment will endanger the future growth rate of the countries, while producing negative effects on the world economy. Non–oil-exporting countries in Latin America comprise a market of more than 360 million people with an average per capita income of about $1,600. For the United States, these countries are more important than the European Economic Community or Japan as consumers of equipment and chemicals, and for the European Economic Community their purchases of those products are nearly as important as those of the United States and more important than those of Japan. Latin America is not neligible as a market for industrial nations; a reversion or substantial weakening of growth rates in the region would affect the world economy. As a consequence of such effect, Latin America would be contributing to unemployment and stagnation in the world economy, which would also affect oil-exporting countries. This effect is small, but it is there. From the point of view of balanced growth in the world economy, current account deficits which are the counterpart of surpluses that would remain as such for a long time, should be financed.

The net amount of resources required is not negligible, since it may involve some $20 to $30 billion per year for non–oil-exporting countries of the region, if allowance is made for the need to increase foreign exchange reserves. These figures do not take into account repayments of foreign debts. If such repayments were included, the figure of gross financial requirements would approach and perhaps exceed $50 billion per year.

These figures, if obtained through borrowing abroad, would imply an increase in global debt (public and private, guaranteed or not) of some 20 percent per year. Up to now the monetary and financial world markets have been able to absorb amounts even higher than these. However, two important points are to be noted. First, the amount of debt a country can manage is not unlimited, and it is lower the shorter the average repayment period; increasing reliance on private bank borrowing will tend to shorten such period. Second, the role industrial countries have played in the supply of financial resources has changed. In the 1960s and early 1970s they transferred abroad part of their own net savings, since they experienced a sustained surplus in their current account balance of payments. In recent years they have functioned as intermediaries for net savings from oil-exporting countries and from a few industrial nations, transferring those savings among themselves and between them and other areas of the world. The figures suggest that recycling foreign savings among themselves is substantially more important than between them and other areas of the world. The latter may be a residual, more volatile figure. Table 8.5 illustrates this assertion.

TABLE 8.5
Estimated Uses of OPEC's Net Contribution
to the European Currency Market (%)

Years	1975	1976	1977	1978	1979	1980
Developing countries	11	10	1	1	14	32
Eastern Europe	36	40	48	74	45	34
Developed countries and rest of the world 1/	53	50	50	25	41	34
Net OPEC contribution	100	100	100	100	100	100
(Billions of dollars)	29	36	38	30	51	76

1. Rest of the world includes off-shore banking centers and unallocated. Insofar as off-shore banking centres orient part of their resources to developing countries, the relative importance of the latter would increase, and th at of the developed countries would diminish.

Sources: Estimated on the basis of data obtained from BIS, *Annual Report* 48 (12 June 1978); *Annual Report* 51 (June 1981).

This analysis is a clear indication that while it is in the interest of Latin America and the world community to finance current account disequilibria of the former group of countries rather than to rely on excessive adjustment, it is also in the interest of all concerned to take a careful look at the form this financing may take. Aside from a reduction in gross reserves, there are two main ways of financing a current account deficit: straight borrowing and direct foreign investment.

Borrowing as a Form of Obtaining Financial Resources

Latin America has increased its reliance on private bank borrowing with the effect of increasing its cost and reducing the repayment period as compared with the situation prevailing in the 1960s. Latin America's recourse to borrowing from official sources, both national and international, has decreased substantially. This change is perhaps irreversible, since there is growing interest in the world to orient low-cost resources to least developed countries of which, according to UN definitions, there is only one in Latin America.

Bank borrowing by developing countries is coming under closer scrutiny, as some banks reach portfolio compositions which include a sizable component of lending to such countries. This development includes the application of some indices to measure credit-worthiness of borrowing countries. The most commonly used indicator of credit-worthiness is the ratio of debt service to exports. The classification of Latin American countries by this indicator shows that countries which register a high ratio of debt service to exports are also among those that enjoy better acceptability as debtors in private financial markets (Argentina, Brazil, Chile, and Uruguay). These data also indicate that countries with high export growth can sustain, unimpaired, a high ratio of debt service to exports.

This particular indicator of credit-worthiness, despite its popularity, does not give an appropriate perspective. It is static and says nothing about export prospects. In the case of most Latin American countries, this indicator might be better interpreted as one of access to foreign credit than as an advanced warning of future trouble (see Table 8.6).

No single indicator, short of a global evaluation of the economic perspectives of a particular country, can give a balanced picture of credit-worthiness. The capacity shown by Latin American countries to weather the difficult economic conditions of the mid-1970s together with their development potential are better clues to the future.

There is a form of borrowing which is becoming increasingly important for a few countries in the region and which is better adapted to their present external financial situation: long-term borrowing from

TABLE 8.6
Non–Oil-Exporting Developing Countries in Latin America: Ratio of Debt Service to Exports and Export Growth Rates (Average of annual ratios, 1971–79)

Country	Ratio of official debt service to exports	Ratio of total debt service to exports	Rate of growth of export
Argentina	19.7	32.0	20.2
Brazil	20.5	48.8	22.5
Chile	23.7	43.0	19.3
Colombia	12.3	22.8	21.6
Costa Rica	12.8	25.1	18.3
Dominican Republic	6.9	16.3	18.5
El Salvador	4.8	13.0	21.5
Guatemala	3.8	9.9	20.2
Guyana	10.3	12.4	8.5
Honduras	6.0	15.1	18.3
Jamaica	9.9	11.4	10.5
Mexico	34.6	41.1	22.6
Nicaragua	13.3	16.3	13.9
Panama	16.5	15.3	13.1
Paraguay	9.9	18.2	25.5
Peru	24.6	42.2	18.2
Uruguay	29.5	33.5	21.5

Sources: ECLA, "Balance of Payments," on the basis of data provided by the IMF, September 1981; IDB, "External Public Debt of the Latin American Countries (Washington, D.C., July 1981).

private capital markets through the sale of bonds. This form of borrowing was already well known in the nineteeth century and developed progressively until the crisis of the 1930s. In recent years only Argentina, Brazil, Mexico, and Venezuela in Latin America have made some use of this means of borrowing. A rapidly growing debt is not a situation Latin American countries consider desirable. Hence, they are increasingly interested in other forms of obtaining financing, including direct foreign investment.

The preceding discussion can be summarized as follows: Non–oil-exporting countries of Latin America have deficits in their current account balance of payments which are substantially larger than those prevailing in previous decades; these deficits are expected to decrease, but still to remain at relatively high levels for several years. Hence, there is a demand for foreign saving both in the form of borrowing and of direct foreign investment. Latin American countries have had, and continue to have, open access to bank borrowing, but these countries would not like to see a foreign debt which continues to rise rapidly and to shorten in terms of maturity. So there is a demand in Latin American countries for longer-term, bonded debt, as well as for direct foreign investment.

Latin America's demand for direct foreign investment is there. The next question to explore is whether it might be interesting to Arab oil-exporting countries to consider expanding their investment portfolio in Latin America. From an economic point of view, direct Arab investments in Latin America could be attractive because of their yields and/or because of their effect on the variability of returns on their investment portfolio as a whole.

Investment Portfolio Diversification:
The Case for Increased Investments in Latin America

International Portfolio Diversification: Economic Advantages

Portfolio diversification to minimize the variance of returns at any given level of the rate of return is common practice. Several models have been developed to provide guidance for the optimal composition of an investment portfolio.[1] International diversification of portfolios is an important dimension of diversification. Rates of return on investment in particular countries will tend to be influenced by the latters' general economic picture. A change in the economic growth rate of any one country will affect rates of return on investment generally. Such influence need not imply perfect correspondence of rates of return in different sectors of the economy. Therefore, there is an advantage in investment diversification even within a country's boundaries.

The fact that different countries' economic growth rates do not move exactly in unison is an indication that rates of return on investments will not all move in the same magnitude or even in the same direction. Even if the average rate of return on investments for all countries were the same, if their movements over time were different, there would be an advantage to international diversification of investments. Such diversification would result in a reduction of the variability of returns on the diversified portfolio for the same level of average returns.

It is general practice in the economic profession to assume that there is a cost attached to uncertainty, so that given any level of returns the investor will prefer lower variability to a higher one. The same argument can be carried over to the situation of a country as a whole. This seems particularly reasonable for countries which are transforming an exhaustible natural resource into a stream of future income. For any given average level of such income, less variability would be preferable to more.

If in order to get higher rates of return on investment, a counrty had to accept larger variability of returns, the choice between possible combinations of average returns on investment and variability would not be obvious. To obtain a higher return, a country would have to accept more variability, and the particular selection would depend on the country's preferences regarding returns and variability as well as on the market opportunities to exchange average return for lower variability. In a case like this it might be advantageous to a country to accept a lower rate of return on its investment portfolio, if that were the cost of a substantially reduced variability of returns. However, if a country or group of countries could obtain higher returns on their investments with the same variability or lower, such a course would be unambiguously preferable to one with lower returns and the same or higher variability.

Average Return and Variance of a Diversified Portfolio

Rates of return on investments in different sectors and countries, developed and developing, have not been at my disposal while writing this chapter. However, as indicated above, a country's economic growth rate exerts a general influence on the rates of return on investment, so that growth rates can be used as a proxy for the rates on investment. Economic theory indicates that under certain circumstances the rate on investment will equal economic growth rate in long-run equilibrium.[2]

Data published by the OECD show that the economic growth rate of member countries as a whole for 1960–80 reached an average of 4.1 percent per year. On the other hand, data published by ECLA show that the economies of the non–oil-exporting countries of Latin America as a whole grew at an average rate of 5.6 percent per year during the same period.[3] If averages per decade are taken, the growth rate of Latin American non-oil-exporting countries was consistently higher than that of OECD countries for the three periods included, the 1950s, 1960s, and 1970s. The variability of the growth rate as measured by the variance was 2.9 for the non–oil-exporting countries of Latin America and 3.7 for OECD during 1950–80 as a whole. The covariance was 0.25 (see Table 8.7).

With these results, it is possible to calculate the average rate of return as well as the variance of a combined portfolio of investments in both areas of the world. Since the average rate of return, as measured by the economic growth rate, is higher for Latin America than for OECD, the combined portfolio will show a higher rate of return than an exclusively OECD portfolio. This is true whatever the relative importance of investments in non–oil-exporting Latin American countries, as long as such relative importance is greater than zero. On the other hand, the variance of the combined portfolio will be smaller, the smaller the covariance of the two series of rates of return.[4]

TABLE 8.7
Growth Rate of Real GDP and Its Variability:
OECD and Non–Oil-Exporting Countries in Latin America (% changes)

Year	Area OECD	Area Latin America	Year	Area OECD	Area Latin America	Year	Area OECD	Area Latin America
1951	7.6	5.7	1961	4.3	6.8	1971	3.7	7.0
1952	3.6	2.6	1962	5.3	3.9	1972	5.4	7.2
1953	4.6	4.7	1963	4.7	3.1	1973	6.1	8.3
1954	1.1	6.0	1964	6.0	7.3	1974	0.6	7.4
1955	7.2	6.2	1965	5.3	5.3	1975	-0.3	3.5
1956	3.2	3.8	1966	5.6	4.6	1976	5.1	5.2
1957	2.8	5.8	1967	3.6	4.3	1977	3.6	4.6
1958	0.6	5.2	1968	5.5	7.0	1978	3.8	5.2
1959	5.6	1.6	1969	4.7	7.4	1979	3.3	6.9
1960	4.5	8.2	1970	3.1	6.9	1980	1.3	6.4
Avg. 51–60	4.1	5.0	Avg. 61–70	4.8	5.7	Avg. 71–80	3.3	6.2

1950 – 1980	OECD	Latin America
Average (%) *	4.1	5.6
Variance	3.7	2.9
Covariance	0.25	
Correlation coefficient	0.08	

* The difference in the averages is statistically significant.

Sources: OECD, *Economic Outlook* (December 1972, 1977; July 1981); ECLA, on the basis of data provided by the reporting countries, as of September 1981.

Assume for example a portfolio in which investments in OECD countries comprised 80 percent of the total, while investments in Latin American countries comprised the remaining 20 percent. The average return on this portfolio would be 4.4 while its variance would be 2.6, which is lower than the variance of both OECD (3.7) and non–oil-exporting Latin American countries (2.9) taken separately. Hence, a diversified portfolio would have a higher yield and a lower variance than an exclusively OECD portfolio. So a diversified portfolio would be unambiguously preferable to a nondiversified OECD one. As the importance of investment in Latin America increases in the combined portfolio, the average return will increase continuously, while the variance will decrease to some minimum point and then increase again.[5]

Optimum Composition of the Investment Portfolio

Using the rates of return, variances, and covariances obtained from growth rate, it is possible to determine the composition of the portfolio that would achieve minimum variance. Such a portfolio would be composed of 44 percent of investment in OECD countries and 56 percent of investments in Latin America, with a variance of 1.7 and an average yield of 4.9 percent. As the importance of Latin America in the investment portfolio continues to increase above 56 percent, the variance would start increasing again from the minimum of 1.7 reached, but it would still be lower than the variance of an investment portfolio in any one of the two areas, until investments in Latin America comprised 100 percent of the total. At that point the variance of the portfolio would be that of returns on investments in Latin America, while the average rate of return would also be that of investments in Latin America.

From the minimum variance portfolio on, further increases of relative importance of investments in Latin America will, as indicated, increase the variance of the combined portfolio, but the rate of return of the portfolio will also increase. So the selection of a particular portfolio composition would depend on relative preferences between rates of return and variances in the investing countries. Instead, the selection of a portfolio composition including investments in Latin America with a relative importance equal to or lower than 56 percent would be unambiguous. Within this limit, a portfolio containing more investments in Latin America would be unambiguously preferred to one containing less, since the former would yield a higher return and a lower variance than the latter.

That data on growth rates that have been used as a proxy for the rates of return on investment conceal several important aspects which should be taken into consideration for an investment decision. First, growth rates in any particular country represent an average of different sectors of the economy. An investor would like to consider the whole set of rates of return rather than only an average, since he might select sectors or projects for his investment among the best available in the economy. Since this is true in both OECD and Latin American countries, the argument for international diversification of the investment portfolio still applies.

Second, the growth rate may be a good proxy of the rate of return on investment in general, including investments such as road construction, education, and other sectors closed to foreign investors. One way to find out whether the growth rate is a reasonable proxy of the rate of return on investments open to foreign investors is to see whether the scanty data available on rates of return on foreign investment behave in a way similar to the growth rates.

The U.S. Department of Commerce publishes figures of the U.S. foreign investment position in different countries and areas of the world, and earnings (after taxes) from those investments from 1967 to 1979.[6] These data should be viewed with care, since earnings can be shifted among affiliates of the same companies in different countries through pricing of products sold or bought among affiliates. This would imply that the variability of earnings appears greater the smaller the amount of investments considered as separate from the global portfolio. Therefore, it should be expected that the variance of the rate of earnings in Latin America, calculated using these data, would increase relative to that of developed countries.

Rate of return calculated using the U.S. Department of Commerce data show that the average rate on U.S. nonoil direct investment abroad is higher for Latin America (13.6 percent) than for developed countries (12.8 percent), while the variances are 5.9 and 6.5 respectively. The covariance is 3.96. Since the rates of return are not corrected for world inflation, they tend to overestimate the real rates.

TABLE 8.8
Rates of Return on U.S. Nonoil Direct Investment Abroad:
Developed Countries and Latin America (%)

Year	Area – Developed Countries	Area – Latin America
1967	9.2	11.3
1968	10.1	12.7
1969	11.4	12.9
1970	10.6	10.8
1971	11.3	9.3
1972	13.0	11.5
1973	15.9	13.5
1974	14.1	16.3
1975	11.7	16.1
1976	12.9	15.0
1977	12.2	14.8
1978	15.6	16.2
1979	18.1	16.7
	Developed Countries	Latin America
Average (%) *	12.8	13.6
Variance	6.50	5.90
Covariance	3.96	
Correlation coefficient	0.64	

* The difference in the average is statistically significant.

Source: Calculated on the basis of U.S. Department of Commerce, *Survey of Current Business* (August 1977-80). Adjusted Earnings divided by the average of the beginning of and end of year Direct Investment Positions.

The variance of the portfolio composed of 80 percent investment in developed countries and 20 percent investments in Latin America would have a rate of return of 13 percent, higher than that of developed countries, and a variance of 5.7, lower than the variance of rates of return on investments in developed countries. The minimum variance portfolio would be comprised of 54 percent investments in Latin America and 46 percent in OECD, with an average yeild of 13.2 percent and a variance of 5.1. Again, as investments in Latin America are increased to over 54 percent of the portfolio, the average return of the portfolio would increase continuously, but the variance would increase also, approaching that of a portfolio composed of investments in Latin America only.

There is an unambiguous advantage to portfolio diversification in favor of Latin America until its participation in the total portfolio reaches 54 percent. From there on, there might also be an advantage, but it would not be unambiguous: it would depend on relative preferences of investing countries between rate of return and variance. The general conclusions obtained using growth rates data as proxy for rates of return on investments are thus strengthened.

Political Risks and the "Mutual Advantages" Approach

Third, neither rates of growth nor of return give a measure of political risks, including capital losses from expropriation. The analysis of the convenience of international portfolio diversification takes into account economic costs and benefits and does not allow for cost arising from political instability. The latter's effect on the rate of return on investments, as distinct from the general effect already reflected in the economic growth rate, boils down to the so-called stability of the rules of the game.

There are two main ways, which are not mutually exclusive, to obtain stability of treatment of foreign investment. One is to have enough influence on the host government so that it will resist pressures for the modification of rules. The other is to make it advantageous for all parties involved not to change the rules. The first way does not operate efficiently, since political power may change hands once in a while in host countries, and foreign influence may become a conflictive issue—as has in fact happened. So the potential influence approach to stability of the rules of the game may be unstable in itself.

The mutual advantage approach has a lot to offer. It uses the criterion of mutual advantage as one important element in the selection of investment projects that can provide such an advantage. For example, development of projects which enhance production in the host country of products that find a market in the investing country or countries may be an important inducement for stability of the rules of the game. The investing country provides both financial resources and markets, so that any element that might negatively affect the investment may also have a negative effect on the buyer markets.

Joint projects undertaken with some equity participation of the host country or countries, and which include international complementarity in production, may also satisfy the criterion of mutual advantage. This latter type of projects implies production of components in more than one country, including the main investor country; it also implies final assembly in more than one country. Though more complex to develop, these projects facilitate access to both the Latin American and the investor countries' markets and permit the undertaking of projects of greater scope, while still satisfying the mutual advantage criterion.

Arab investment providing both financial resources and markets will be less vulnerable than if the provision of only financial resources were involved. This vulnerability would be reduced even further if a mechanism could be stablished for Arab oil-exporting countries to invest as a group rather than individually. By acting as a group, since Arab countries have different political orientations, they would offer the host countries a possibility of diversification of their political portfolio, thus reducing the political risks that come as a byproduct of political conflict. From the point of view of Latin America, a wider nationality diversification in foreign investment would certainly be welcome.

The Magnitudes Involved: Are They Bearable?

At present annual investment rates, non–oil-exporting countries of Latin America are investing some $100 billion annually, of which less than 5 percent represents direct foreign investment. If Arab oil-exporting countries decided to invest in Latin America one-fifth of their flow of long-term investment abroad per year, this would mean about one-eighth of their current account surpluses and about 4 percent of total annual investment in Latin America.[7] Figures of this order of magnitude should not create any absorption problem in the area unless they were concentrated in one or two countries. This latter possibility does not necessarily maximize the benefits of international portfolio diversification. So the global magnitudes of investment that would help obtain the benefits of international diversification of the portfolio do not seem, at least from a global point of view, difficult to assimilate in the area.

The next question is whether there are specific investment opportunities which could provide the advantages of diversification from the Arab countries' point of view and which would also be advantageous from a Latin American point of view, while containing elements which could induce stability in the treatment of foreign investment in the host countries. An answer to this question would require a more detailed look at the economy of various Latin American countries, and this is beyond the scope of this chapter. However, a general review of these problems may disclose the existence of areas of common interest.

One of the most difficult problems Latin America continues to face is an accelerated rate of rural-urban migration. This tends to aggravate both economic and social problems: urban unemployment is high, while housing, transportation, sanitation, and other services are overburdened by the rapid increase of population. At the same time, an abundant resource in the region is left underutilized: agricultural land.

The development of agricultural and agroindustrial production exports is of substantial interest for Latin America. The production of wheat, corn, soybeans, beef and mutton, sugar, coffee and tobacco, as well as fruits, vegetables, and their pulps and juices, could be advantageously expanded. Timber, wood products, pulp and paper, shoes, and cotton and wool textiles are among other interesting possibilities. Taking advantage of the mineral raw materials existing in the region, several products such as copper wire and pipes, and a wide variety of goods in the light industrial field, could be advantageously manufactured in the area. All these products could find a market in oil-exporting countries and other countries in the Arab world.

Latin America needs both financial resources and foreign markets to continue growing, and the Arab oil-exporting countries could provide both. A program of cooperation involving Arab investment in the production of commodities destined to Arab markets could benefit all parties involved. For Latin America the advantages would be in the further development of its agriculture and industry, thus helping to stop the fast rate of rural-urban migration and alleviating unemployment or hidden unemployment; assisting in the continued diversification of exports, thus increasing both the level and stability of foreign exchange inflows with a positive effect on the stability of foreign finances and of the economy as a whole; and contributing to sustained overall economic growth. For Arab oil-exporting countries the economic advantages would be in the security of supply of a wide variety of products and the attractive rates of return on investments in the market where such products come from. Analysis of the political advantages is outside our present scope.

Institutional Arrangements for Cooperation

Apart from direct investments there are many other areas of financial cooperation between Arab oil-exporting countries and Latin America. Latin America is interested in longer-term borrowing, so that an expanded access of Latin American countries to the capital markets of oil-exporting countries would certainly be welcome. However, this area of cooperation may be more difficult to develop, since the differential rates of return for investing countries of Latin America or other financial investments would not be substantial. Here the main advantages would be, from the investor's point of view, in spreading political risks, a subject not explored here.

Oil-exporting countries have already been contributing to facilities in the IMF and the World Bank, and such contributions are also important to Latin America. There is an important gap at present in financial facilities available to Latin America countries, which is the lack of arrangements that supply credit in the five to ten years maturity range. This gap could be filled either through contributions to the IDB or through setting up a special facility for the purpose.

Our main conclusion is that it would be in the interest of Arab oil-exporting countries to diversify their direct investment portfolio toward Latin America. This requires a conscious effort of exploring specific investment opportunities in particular areas in different countries. Despite the fact that in most Latin American countries Arab immigration has been important in the past, information on investment opportunities which might be of interest to Arab countries is not easily available. Hence, if there is a decision to diversify their investment portfolio, it should be accompanied by a systematic effort to find the specific investments or projects which would be undertaken. Such effort requires organization.

The recent establishment of the Arab Latin American Bank with capital from several Arab and Latin American countries may provide a base to undertake the required studies. Arab contributions to the bank come from only a few countries, and that might be a somewhat narrow base. A special project under UN auspices could perhaps provide a wider base to explore investment possibilities of mutual interest to Arab and Latin American countries. Whatever the arrangements, the important aspect to be underlined is that investment portfolio diversification cannot be achieved without the cost of a systematic effort of exploration of investment opportunities.

Notes

I gratefully acknowledge comments from Norberto González and statistical assistance from Tatjana Montes and María Arce. The opinions expressed here are my sole responsibility and in no way commit the institutions with which I am affiliated.

1. See H.G. Grubel, "Internationally Diversified Portfolios: Welfare Gains and Capital Flows," *American Economic Review* 58 (1968):1299-1314.

2. See Harry G. Johnson, *Macroeconomics and Monetary Theory* (London: Lowe & Brydone, 1971), ch. 20.
3. These figures correspond to a weighted average of the growth rate of gross domestic product of each country, using the GDP as weights.
4. The variance of the combined portfolio is obtained from: $S^2 (A,B) = a^2 S^2 (A) + (1-a)^2 S^2 (B) + a(1 - a) S(A) (B)$, where $S^2 (A)$ and $S^2 (B)$ are the variances of each of the series of returns and $S (A) (B)$ is the covariance. The weights are a and $(1-a)$.
5. This chapter takes broad economic areas as a whole without exploring diversity within them. This approach, which would be erroneous if one attempted to describe the areas in question, is still useful to tackle problems of international diversification of investments. The fact that each area is composed of different economic units that behave differently is already taken into consideration in the calculation of the average growth rate and of variances and covariances. Obviously, if economic policy decisions were taken by each area as a unit, their interaction would be higher than it is at present and the covariance calculated would also be higher, reducing the advantages of international investment diversification.
6. U.S. Department of Commerce, *Survey of Current Business*, August 1977, table 12; August 1980.
7. These figures assume a flow of long-term investments abroad by Arab oil-exporting countries of $20 billion per year, and a current account surplus of $32 billion.

9
The Quest for
A New International Economic Order of
the Oceans: A Case of Arab-Latin
American Cooperation

Francisco Orrego Vicuna

The Arab and Latin American countries share a tradition of understanding and cooperation in international forums on major issues of international concern. This fruitful cooperation in multilateral diplomacy is evidenced by their common positions on political and economic matters in the United Nations, whether at the various UN Conferences on Trade and Development (UNCTAD), the North-South dialogue,[1] or the Law of the Sea conferences. In addition, political, economic, and cultural relations are increasing between Arab and Latin American countries.

The Third Conference on the Law of the Sea provided a unique opportunity to further this tradition into new areas of international action, in which vital interests of both groups of countries are dramatically involved. The leadership of Arab and Latin American countries in this area of international diplomacy has proven a decisive factor in Third world solidarity and a key element in the power struggle between industrialized and developing countries.

At present, the significance of the Law of the Sea negotiations lies beyond the formal aspect of reviewing some classic definitions of jurisdiction over the seas or drafting treaty articles which might improve existing conventions and customary rules. The fundamental issues under negotiation refer to the policies on natural resources and raw materials that are part of the broader field of international economic relations and the complex rearrangements being sought within the New International Economic Order.

The Law of the Sea has become the first subject where the new principles, institutions, and goals of the New International Economic

Order could be agreed upon, enacted, and implemented at the international level. This means that the outcome of the Conference on the Law of the Sea will also influence other negotiations and processes presently developing in a variety of forums.

Two substantive issues are predominant in the context of the conference and constitute paramount examples of fruitful Arab–Latin American cooperation. The first refers to the economic jurisdiction of coastal states over their natural resources within the 200-mile Exclusive Economic Zone and the continental shelf. The second and most important issue refers to the exploitation of the seabed mineral resources beyond the limits of national jurisdiction.

The 200-Mile Policy: Permanent Sovereignty over the Resources of Adjacent Seas

Since its enactment by Chile in 1947, the principle of the 200-mile economic zone quickly gained acceptance throughout Latin America[2] and was soon incorporated into the laws and policies of most Third World countries. This principle embodied a basic concept of economic justice, which ensured its success and recognition by the community of nations. It proclaimed the right of coastal states to the resources of adjacent seas and the prevention of their depletion by distant fishing states which had stretched the freedom of the high seas beyond reasonable limits.

This claim by developing countries—later accepted and implemented by the industrialized countries themselves—was the first step toward establishing the concept of permanent sovereignty over natural resources as it developed in the 1960s. Coastal states reaffirmed their sovereignty and jurisdiction over living and nonliving resources within the 200-mile zone. The economic aspect of the claim was the essential factor which inspired the principle and established it as a policy. This also explains why this policy was supported by both Latin American and Arab countries, in spite of the different geographic characteristics of each region.[3]

Most Latin American countries have long coastlines facing the open seas, which made it easier for them to adopt the 200-mile principle. In the case of Arab countries, geography determined their short coastlines, enclosed and semienclosed seas, and other features comparatively much more complex in relation to the 200-mile zone. To a great extent, these differences are also true with regard to the continental shelf. These differences notwithstanding, the Arab countries strongly supported the 200-mile principle in their opening statements, which were made at the first session of the Law of the Sea Conference held in Caracas in 1974.[4] This Arab position has since remained, without variation, in keeping with the Latin American position all along the negotiation process.[5]

To support a principle does not necessarily mean that all the countries concerned should agree on all the detailed provisions through which this principle is expressed. National interests bear a strong influence on the determination of particular modalities of a given institution, while keeping with the basic and fundamental common objectives. In the negotiation process, the Arab countries emphasized different aspects of the Exclusive Economic Zone with a view to accommodate the national problems arising from particular situations. Special circumstances such as islands, straits used for international navigation, shelf configuration, roles for delimitation, and geographically disadvantaged status, were put forward by one or another Arab country in seeking to preserve their national interests. The same is true with regard to Latin American countries, where national interests were expressed in different manners, ranging from broad and narrow shelf conditions to the situation of land-locked countries, and including every possible special circumstance that the seas have known.

This legitimate exercise at diversity has in no way constituted an obstacle to the pursuit of the common goal of establishing the 200-mile Exclusive Economic Zone. Arab–Latin American solidarity was strong enough to ensure success and resist divisionary tactics by countries which have refused to admit the progress of history and the corresponding change of conditions rapidly taking place.

Arab and Latin American countries, together with other developing countries, are now able to control the natural resources of the maritime areas adjacent to their respective territories. The establishment of this principle took thirty years of continuous struggle to materialize, but it is now a firm and positive proof of the capacity of developing countries to bring about substantive changes in international economic relations and in the disposition of raw materials and other resources.

Seabed Mineral Exploitation: The Arab–Latin American Experience

Exploitation of seabed mineral resources has become the most important issue to be discussed in the international economic field, partly because of the influence that resulting solutions will have on many other definitions and subjects in the years ahead. Again in this field, Arab–Latin American cooperation has been a decisive factor in the negotiation process, since each region has a unique experience in mining and oil production and in the related problems of management, investment negotiation, commercialization, taxation, etc. The international regime for the exploitation of seabed resources deals with the most extensive mineral operation ever undertaken, and therefore reproduces on a larger and more difficult scale all the problems and situations which have risen at the national level.

Resolution 2749 (XXV), passed by the UN General Assembly in 1970, solved the first basic question that lies at the heart of any acceptable regime, by declaring the seabed area beyond the limits of national jurisdiction and its resources as the common heritage of mankind. For the first time the concept of common property of resources was introduced in the international community. It followed that the management and exploitation of such resources could only be organized under an international regime, thus posing the complex question of how and under what rules this regime should be established and developed.

Although the technical factors explain to some extent the difficulties and complexities of this effort, the fundamental problem is related to the different interests which developed and developing countries have in the matter. Developed countries have a major strategic interest in the seabed minerals to ensure secure sources of supply and reduce their growing deficit in raw materials. This interest—even stronger than that in the expected profitability of their investments—is clearly revealed in the following table:

Industrialized Countries' Imports as a Percentage of Consumption of Four Basic Minerals

	United States	European Economic Community	Japan
Manganese	98	99	86
Nickel	72	100	100
Copper	6	96	83
Cobalt	96	100	100

Source: Herman Kahn, *The Next 200 Years* (New York: Macmillan), 1967, p. 97, table 7.

In relation to these large deficits industrialized countries have sought a free and unimpeded access to such minerals and a restricted role for the proposed international authority. In a sense, the same philosophy on which these countries base their national economies is projected to the seabed regime. For developing countries, however, the nature of the problem is entirely different. The exploitation of a common heritage of mankind must benefit mankind as a whole and not only those countries which have the capital and technology to undertake seabed mining. Therefore, the international regime must provide specific conditions and requirements which will govern exploitation, and the authority must be able to control all mining activities in the area.

The national experiences of developing countries in the field of mining and resource exploitation have called for a fundamental evolution in the kinds of mining contracts and conditions which also must be taken into account by the seabed regime.[6] It would be unrealistic to base a new and pioneering international regime on concession models of mining which have been surpassed in international and domestic practice.[7]

Many developing countries are present or potential land-based producers of the minerals concerned and can be faced with a serious competition from seabed exploitation which would adversely affect their exports and earnings. Production control is an essential element in the international regime, which collides with the unrestricted freedom sought by industrialized countries.

These important differences are evidenced in the discussion of three basic issues: the system of exploitation, the resource policy, and the financial arrangements of contracts. These issues, which will be examined next, are parts of the New International Economic Order and are strongly influenced by the Arab and Latin American experiences.

System of Exploitation:
Modern Contracts versus Traditional Concessions

The first approach of the industrialized countries with regard to the exploitation system was to set up an international authority whose powers would be limited to granting and registering seabed mining licenses under a procedure of automatic processing. This was equivalent to the most classical models of mining concession with a strong resemblance to colonial mining rights.[8]

The developing countries supported a system in which exploitation would be directly undertaken by the international authority through the enterprise as its operational body. Within its discretionary powers the authority would authorize operations by private or state entities in the area. From this perspective, the authority would become the functional equivalent of the state in administering mining operations in its territory under the principle of permanent sovereignty over natural resources.[9]

The compromise formula called for the establishment of a parallel system in which both the authority and private or state operators would be entitled to undertake mining activities in the area. Under this system, private and state operators would have guaranteed access to the resources of the area if they qualified in terms of technical, operational, financial, and other requirements. This access would not be automatic, since applicants would have to negotiate with the authority certain key aspects of their contracts, including financial contributions and transfers of technology.

The operation of the system would require that each applicant for a contract propose to the authority two mining sites of equivalent commercial value, of which it would grant one as the contract area and reserve the other for its own direct exploitation or for preferential exploitation by developing countries. Joint ventures, service contracts, production sharing schemes, and other forms of association would also be possible with regard to one or the other site.[10]

Although the proposed compromise is imaginative in its effort to accommodate the basic interests of developed and developing countries, many issues are still to be solved before it becomes an acceptable solution. The most important of these is how to ensure that the enterprise will in fact become an operational reality able to undertake mining activities.

Financing of the enterprise is the first important question. Ideas have ranged from compulsory contributions by states to other means of capital formation. While it is not difficult to secure financing for the first operation of the enterprise, the question remains as to how to finance the following operations in order to keep the system really parallel.

The second important question relates to the technological capability of the enterprise. Ideas have ranged from compulsory transfer of technology, as a condition for awarding contracts, to the enactment of programs which would encourage such a transfer on a voluntary basis and which could eventually provide financial incentives. In any event, it is inescapable that the enterprise will need the necessary technology to operate.

Many other problems remain unresolved. The information the applicant should give the authority about the parallel sites has proven an important question. Developing countries have insisted that such sites should be previously explored by the applicant, while developed countries are willing to prospect only before the contract is actually awarded. Antimonopoly clauses, and eventually a system of quotas, are yet to be discussed, among many other issues.

The complexity of any such system requires a strong authority with all the necessary powers to regulate operations, control activities, and ensure compliance with the rules. Differences are also evident in this regard, particularly in terms of the composition of the organs and their respective powers. Whatever the final solution, one fundamental policy is already firmly established: the system of exploitation will not constitute a mining concession and, to a large extent, will incorporate the modern view of mining contracts which developing countries—Arab and Latin American in particular—have developed through their experience.

It is possible that any agreed-upon system might be conceived as a provisional regime with a duration of twenty or twenty-five years at the end of which the experience would be evaluated and the regime modified accordingly. In one suggested alternative, exploitation would revert to the authority at the end of such period, following the precedent of some oil-exploitation contracts.

Adverse Effects on Land-Based Mining

One of the most difficult issues under consideration is the resource policy of the authority, with particular reference to the prevention of adverse economic effects on land-based producers of the minerals concerned. Since production control is an essential element of this policy—which requires some degree of planning—it conflicts with the economic philosophy of industrialized countries.

Industrialized countries have argued for many years that no adverse economic effects would result from seabed mining. Evidence to the contrary is alarmingly strong. A recent UN study has shown that by the year 2000 some 60.6 percent of the world nickel demand would be supplied by seabed mining. The figures are 150 percent for cobalt and 93.7 percent for manganese.[11] In the case of copper, 7 percent of world demand could be supplied by seabed mining, but since developing countries supply 39 percent of world demand, the impact has to be measured relative to their share of the market. In this case seabed mining could represent 18 percent of world demand. Because of this situation and the adverse effect on prices it will generate, a recent UNCTAD study has estimated that exports income of copper-producing developing countries would diminish by the year 2000 to about $2.4 billion.[12] This explains why developing countries, in a most impressive demonstration of solidarity with land-based producers, have insisted on the inclusion of appropriate measures to prevent such adverse effects. UN General Assembly Resolution 2749, as well as several UNCTAD resolutions and declarations of regional groups of developing countries, has emphasized the need to prevent these adverse effects.

Three specific mechanisms for prevention have been agreed upon so far, although many important details are still pending. The first mechanism is the conclusion of long-term commodity agreements to regulate the international market for such minerals. These agreements would ensure price stability, adequate supplies, limits on production, and eventually, regulatory stocks. The authority would participate in such agreements for seabed production, although the extent of such participation is still a matter of controversy. UNCTAD would be the appropriate body for the negotiation of these agreements.

The second and most important mechanism is to put limits on seabed production which would be in force until the long-term commodity agreements referred to above enter into force. Industrialized countries have strongly opposed this mechanism as a matter of principle, but since 1976 have accepted to discuss some of its aspects. Some proposals have suggested as a limit the whole projected cumulative growth segment of the world nickel market. This meant that land-based production would have no share in the growth of the world market. The Group of 77 has suggested as a limit 50 percent of such growth. Other proposals have mentioned figures in between.

Although the nickel standard also applies to copper, it does not necessarily cover manganese, cobalt, or other minerals which could be produced from the seabed. The Group of 77 has suggested the establishment of a separate limit for each mineral to take care, on a case-by-case basis, of the different situations which might arise. In all cases, however, an economic planning commission would conduct studies and recommend appropriate measures. Appropriate production limits are still under negotiation, including the technical details for their calculation and operation. It is now clear that there will be limits on ocean production which will guard effectively against adverse economic effects on the land-based producers.

The third mechanism is compensatory in nature. It seeks to indemnify the land-based producers who would suffer because of seabed production where preventive measures would be ineffective. The solidarity of the Group of 77 has been crucial in the negotiations. Most developing countries are actual or potential producers of the minerals concerned and are threatened by the adverse effects that may result from seabed mining. Today it may be nickel, copper, manganese, or cobalt; tomorrow it might be any other mineral the seabed can produce, including oil.

Financial Provisions: Influence of the Oil and Mining Experiences

The financial arrangements of contracts are the third major issue which has divided developed and developing countries. Again, this is an area where Arab–Latin American cooperation has been extremely useful in the negotiation process. The problems underlying this area are almost identical to those present in the relationships between the state and foreign investors in the mining sector.[13]

It has now been firmly established, as a basic principle, that contractors will be required to share part of their profits with the authority. An international taxation policy is being developed to that effect. It would be desirable that the financial terms of contracts be defined, on a case-by-case basis, through negotiations, since the experience of developing countries indicates that each multinational corporation has a different motive for investing, and therefore its financial contribution might be higher or lower. Also, the debt/equity ratio is different in each case, and the discounted cash flow, among other factors, justifies different financial treatments. Industrialized countries have argued in favor of defining financial arrangements in the convention itself. This proposition would result in avoiding competition among applicants and restrict the power of negotiation of the authority, which would then be limited to the negotiation of joint ventures, incentives for the transfer of technology, and other specific aspects.

Agreement has been made about a profit-sharing scheme in which the percentage of the authority's participation would increase along with the profits, thus taking care of windfall profits situations.[14] However, specific figures have not yet been agreed upon. In view of their experience in oil exploitation, developing countries have required additional financial charges, such as royalties collected independently from profits and which assign a value to the resources in situ (the preferred modality would be a percentage of the value of processed metals in the market), and site rentals and equivalent charges. These charges would avoid speculation with site holdings. Beyond the specific level of financial charges and their modalities, a number of other important aspects require detailed consideration:

1. The authority will have to observe strict accounting practices to eliminate overpricing of certain factors such as technology, or underpricing others such as sales between subsidiaries.[15]
2. The case of socialist countries, where no market prices or profit concepts are used, will present some difficulties in developing a profit-sharing scheme. A posted price system, such as the one used in oil exploitation, has been suggested as a solution.
3. The most difficult problem relates to the stages that would be subject to such a scheme of profit-sharing. The process of exploitation, as conceived by the developing countries, is an indivisible whole which includes the processing of minerals and the sale of the resulting metals. Therefore all profits obtained during the process are subject to share or taxation. The developed countries have argued that only the stage of extraction is subject to this scheme, while the processing and following phases are subject to domestic taxation under national jurisdiction. It follows that the authority would be deprived from sharing in the most significant profits —those produced at the end of the process.

Financial charges should be defined in such a way as not to discourage production, but they should not be so generous as to deprive the authority from its legitimate share or to provoke a situation of unbalance with regard to the financial conditions prevailing in land-based mining. Otherwise, investments would all go to seabed mining in prejudice of land production.

Conclusion: An Arab–Latin American Reminder

An entirely new model of resource development is being defined at the Law of the Sea Conference, as a first step toward the establishment of the New International Economic Order. Arab and Latin American countries have contributed their experiences in this field by safeguarding the rights of the owners of natural resources and allowing a fair treatment of those investing their capital and technology in the exploitation of such resources.

In spite of efforts being made to ensure a balanced and just system, some powerful corporate and political interests in some developed countries are pressing for unilateral national legislation to undertake exploitation of the seabed resources on their own with no regard to international negotiations. Such legislation would constitute a serious violation of international law and would irreparably damage the progress of negotiations at the conference. Should such a situation arise, Arab and Latin American countries would have to consider countermeasures to safeguard their interests as well as those of other developing countries. Experience is also at hand to deal with this eventuality.

Notes

1. For Arab–Latin American cooperation within the framework of the North-South dialogue, see United Nations, Report on the Conference on International Economic Cooperation, Document E 1 L. 17748, July 1977.
2. Presidential proclamation of June 23, 1947, establishing a 200-mile Zone of Maritime Jurisdiction.
3. For geographic and other factors revelant to the Law of the Sea including Arab and Latin American countries, see John King Gamble, Jr., *Global Marine Attributes* (Cambridge, Mass.: Ballinger, 1974).
4. United Nations, Third United Nations Conference on the Law of the Sea, Official Record, vol. 1. See in particular the statements by the following Arab countries: Egypt (p. 75), Yemen (p. 116), the Arab League (p. 119), Democratic Republic of Yemen (p. 125), United Arab Emirates (p. 141), Saudi Arabia (p. 144), Iraq (p. 148), Oman (p. 152), Tunisia (p. 153), Somalia (p. 186), Palestine Liberation Organization (p. 191), Lebanon (p. 135), Libya (p. 132), and Kuwait (p. 155).

5. See Francisco Orrego Vicuna, *Las políticas latinoamericanas sobre el derecho del mar: perspectivas de un acuerdo general de transacción* (Santiago de Chile: Universidad de Chile, Departamento de Estudios Internacionales, 1976).
6. See in general, David Nathan Smith and Louis T. Wells, Jr., *Negotiating Third World Mineral Agreements* (Cambridge, Mass.: Ballinger, 1975).
7. For this changing practice see Henry Cattan, *The Law of Oil Concessions in the Middle East and North Africa* (New York: Oceana, 1967).
8. On traditional concessions see Smith and Wells, p. 31.
9. UNGA Resolution 1803 (XVII), December 14, 1962.
10. For the new kind of agreements, particularly in the oil industry, see Smith and Wells, p. 37; Robert Fabrikant, "Production Sharing Contracts in the Indonesian Petroleum Industry," *Harvard International Law Journal* 16 (1975):303.
11. Jean Pierre Levy, "Importancia de los recursos minerales de los fondos marinos y estado de la tecnología de la minería marina en aguas profundas," *Economía de los Océanos*, UN Economic Commission for Latin America, 1977, p. 123, table 7.
12. Bernard G. Marin-Curtoud, "Consecuencias económicas de la explotación de los recursos minerales de los océanos," ibid., p. 144.
13. See Smith and Wells, ch. 3, on financial provisions; Charles J. Lipton, *Fiscal Aspects of Negotiating Third World Mineral Development Agreements* (New York: United Nations Center on Transnational Corporations, document no. 8, 1977).
14. On this kind of scheme see Stephen Zorn, *Renegotiating Mining Agreements: The Case of Bougainville Copper* (New York: UN Center on Transnational Corporations, document no. 15, 1977).
15. United Nations, *The Impact of Multinational Corporations on Development and on International Relations* (New York, 1974).

10

Toward a Constructive Dialogue between Arab and Latin American Countries

Hussain Khallaf

The inflation of a dialogue between the Arab and Latin American countries acquires special importance in light of contemporary international developments and changing circumstances in both regions. This dialogue should be examined in the context of the following considerations:

- The recent orientation of the Arab countries to hold meetings and dialogues with other regional and international groups. Such meetings and dialogues (Afro-Arab and Euro-Arab dialogues) have covered economic and political matters of common concern.
- The modern international trend toward economic and political regrouping that is characteristic of the present age in which small entities are losing importance, particularly in technological innovations.
- Current efforts of developing countries, including the Arab and Latin American countries, to rectify the economic and political conditions imposed on them during past centuries of military and economic imperialism. Such conditions have placed developing countries in a position in which their natural and economic resources are under-utilized. This has made it possible for these resources to be exploited by industrialized countries. Such exploitation has occurred either directly or indirectly through multinational corporations.

The efforts of developing countries to rectify their political and economic relations with the industrialized countries have resulted in the passage of two documents by the UN General Assembly, one regarding the establishment of a New International Economic Order and the other regarding a Program of Action. The establishment of OPEC by a group of developing countries to defend their petroleum interests has been equally instrumental in making the industrialized countries mindful of the importance of initiating a dialogue with the developing countries. Other international meetings and conferences between the developing and industrialized countries have sought to rectify international economic relations, particularly in the areas of international trade, international monetary transactions, technology transfer, and economic assistance.

The Arab countries have emphasized the importance of continuing efforts to rectify international economic relations and restrain monopolistic international controls. In doing so they have sought to build bridges of cooperation with other developing countries, including those of Latin America. Cooperation between the Arab and Latin American countries is made necessary by the international economic conditions cited above, as well as by the great similarities of their economic, social, and political conditions. The common denominator of both groups of countries is manifested in the similarity of their economic structures, the prevalence of the same economic and social conditions, and the attention given in both to economic and social development.

Considering the progress achieved in both regions and the aspiration for similiar development goals, it is possible that development experiences could be shared and cooperation in economic, social, cultural, and political matters could be strengthened. This cooperation would help realize the developmental goals that the peoples in both regions, as well as other peoples in the Third World, have always aspired to in facing their common destiny. In this chapter I shall discuss the economic structures of both the Arab and Latin American groups of countries, their political and economic importance, and their curent relations and the measures that could be adopted to develop them.

Economic Structures

The Arab and Latin American economies have tremendous natural and human resources that can be used rationally to reset their equilibrium and to stamp out underdevelopment. The Arab world produces about 33.4 percent of total world output of oil and has half the world reserves. In addition to a number of other important resources, such as natural gas, phosphate, copper, and iron ore, there are agricultural resources which, if properly developed, can meet the needs of the region and leave surpluses for export. The Latin American countries also have mineral resources such as iron ore, copper, oil, and gas, and agricultural resources such as sugar, cotton, coffee, and fruits, which constitute a high percentage of world production.

In terms of human resources, the population of the Arab world is now 160 million, or 4.3 percent of world population, and it is expected to reach 200 million by the year 2000. The population of Latin America is now 345 million, or 8.5 percent of world population, and it is expected to reach 600 million by the year 2000. In both regions the labor force is about 20-25 percent of the total population, compared to 40-50 percent of the developed countries.

Total Arab production in 1977 was $167 billion, or 2.5 percent of total world production. Total Latin American production was $360 billion, or 5.4 percent of total world production. Annual growth rates in both regions were similar to those in the Third World, reaching 4-6 percent. Two other phenomena are evident in both regions: one is the disparity of growth rates from one country to another; the second is the disparity of per capita income in the countries themselves. In 1977, the annual growth rate in the oil-producing countries reached 30 percent, and per capita income ranged from $70 to $14,000.

The structure of the Arab and Latin American economies is also similar in that both are concentrated in the primary sectors (extraction and agriculture) which amount to 60-70 percent of total GNP. The industrial sector's contribution is minimal, hardly reaching 20 percent of total GNP in the most developed countries of both regions.

The Arab world contributes 5-7 percent of total world exports and 4-5 percent of total world imports. Arab exports amount to 60-65 percent of total domestic production, of which 85-90 percent are exports from the primary sectors. Industrial goods amount to 70-75 percent of total Arab imports. Total Arab trade with European and Latin American countries, both import and export, amounts to 6 percent of total world trade. The structure of Latin American foreign trade closely resembles that of the Arab world.

Social and Cultural Similarities

As both the Arab and Latin American countries belong to the Third World, they share similar conditions of social and economic under-development. Underdevelopment is a common heritage in both regions, and it is manifested in low productivity, high illiteracy and unemployment, deficient health and educational services, and inadequate transportation, communication, and housing. These conditions are strengthened by the prevalence of custom and tradition: family ties, hierarchical class structure, maldistribution of property, disrespect for industrial work, low social status for women, weak governmental administration, and a multiplicity of conflicting laws and regulations. To these conditions are added high birth and mortality rates, insufficient awareness of development and technological know-how, and deficient statistical methods which weaken the government's ability for economic and social planning.

Despite geographic distance and the language difference of the two regions, the roots of both Arabs and Latin Americans are to be found in the Iberian Peninsula, where their blood mixed for many centuries during the reign of the Andalusian Arab state. During that period Arabic and Spanish borrowed many of their words and meanings from each other, and the interaction of both peoples marked their social customs and traditions. Many of their innovations profoundly influenced and even accelerated the development of Western civilization. There is no better indication of the deep social and cultural ties between the peoples of the two regions today than the existence of more than ten million descendants of Arab origin in Latin American countries.

Political and Economic Importance

The Arab world occupies a strategic geographic location as a center of communication between three continents, as well as the region where more than half of the world oil reserves are found. These two assets have made the region a target of imperialist greed for many centuries, culminating in the establishment of a Zionist entity in the heart of the Arab world. The presence of this entity was intended to frustrate the liberation of the region from its colonial ties and maintain its fragmentation.

Similarly, Latin America plays an important role in world politics, whether because of its strategic location between the world's oceans, connecting the West with the Far East, or because of its economic and political potential. Latin America is no less important than the Arab world, because it contains many of the essential minerals and agricultural crops which increasingly play important roles in the productive machinery of the modern world.

The Arab and Latin American countries constitute important markets for the products of the industrialized countries. Both regions contain 12.8 percent of the world population and contribute about 9 percent to total world production. They are considered strategic political and economic targets of international imperialism and multinational corporations, which for many years have had a tight grip on their economies and have reduced them to subservience in the world's overall production, trade, and finance. The two groups of countries were subjected to military occupation for many years, and their resources suffered extensive exploitation. In spite of their political independence a new form of colonialism, manifested in the West's economic hegemony, continues to deepen its roots in their economies.

Arab–Latin American Economic Relations

In spite of the traditionally small volume of trade between the Arab world and Latin America, this volume has increased from $330 million in 1971, to $1.31 billion in 1976. Arab exports increased from $270 million in 1971 to $1.02 billion in 1976. Equally, Arab imports from Latin America increased from $60 million to $295 million in the same period. The principal commodities exported are petroleum, phosphates, natural gas, fertilizers, and textiles. The principal commodities imported are sugar, coffee, meat, cereals, vegetables, fruits, tea, spices, cocoa, and tobacco. Most of the commodities exchanged between the two regions are extractive and agricultural products, with some manufactured goods, to meet the needs of local markets. These commodities are not produced locally or are produced in insufficient quantitites to meet local demand.

Present circumstances seem to force the two groups of countries to continue their patterns of trade with developed countries in the area of industrial goods, unless some necessary changes are made in the structure of their economic relations. It is through this structuring process that their industrial sectors could be pushed ahead to a more balanced position with other sectors. This objective could not be accomplished without some strenuous efforts inside each group of countries. These efforts would be greatly helped by the cooperation of those developed countries which have the ability and desire to help developing countries by offering them scientific and technological know-how. This calls for the coordination of positions by the parties willing to contribute to such an endeavor.

Pushing ahead with industrialization need not depend on aid from developed countries as much as on self-help. Not all Arab and Latin American countries have equal standing in terms of scientific and technological progress, quantitatively and qualitatively. Some countries have already achieved significant progress and accumulated sufficient experience to be used by other countries in both regions. It is also possible to take advantage of the present capital surplus funds of some OPEC countries. A significant part of these surpluses has been invested in Western financial institutions for reinvestment in developing countries. OPEC countries have also offered other Third World countries aid and loans, and these can play an important role in future relations between the two regions.

Development of Arab–Latin American Relations

In light of this discussion and the necessity of establishing close cooperation between the Arab and Latin American groups of countries, it is timely to begin weaving the treads of such cooperation. Otherwise, future generations will be condemned to remain in their present state of economic and social underdevelopment. Furthermore, our civilization—the basis of Western civilization—would remain in the traps of colonialism. Assuming the similarity of political and economic conditions in both regions and convinced that such conditions ought to be changed, we specify our objectives in cooperation as follows:

- Adopting complementary development strategies and economic plans to break free from economic dependency on industrialized countries. This requires an effort to restructure the economies of both regions so as to enable them to deal with each other on equitable bases.
- Initiating scientific and technological cooperation between the two regions.
- Increasing the volume of trade, not only in traditional commodities but also in commodities which could be planned for future production in both regions.
- Eliminating trade barriers between the two regions, expanding transportation and communication systems, facilitating the exchange of information, granting exemptions and favorable tariffs, and easing administrative requirements.
- Fostering the development of social and cultural relations by increasing the interaction of popular organizations and unions in both regions.

The point of departure in such cooperation is the initiation of an Arab–Latin American dialogue which includes economic, social, political, and cultural relations. This dialogue may be based on the following principles:

- The equality of both the Arab and Latin American groups of countries.
- The desire to crystallize and establish a new economic and political model for all developing countries which lays the foundations of their cooperation vis-à-vis the developed countries. This model must

permit each developing country to improve its position in light of its economic, political, and social conditions.

- The desirability of cooperation between the Arab and Latin American groups of countries, particularly in the economic area, to permit the full development of their economies.
- The need for establishing a mechanism to coordinate their political and economic policies, both regionally and internationally.

Organizationally, the most important areas which could be conceived in the first stage of the dialogue are the following:

- Exploring the economic interests of the Arab and Latin American countries and reviewing their experiences within the framework of the League of Arab States and the Organization of American States. Periodic meetings could be held in which Arabs and Latin Americans participate to exchange ideas and experiences and to use them in formulating strategies for economic and social development in both regions.
- Bringing together chambers of commerce from both regions to help develop trade relations, study the problems and restrictions that impede trade development, and recommend the necessary measures to alleviate them.
- Developing Arab–Latin American friendship associations to encourage cooperation in educational, social, and sports activities.
- Taking advantage of OPEC capital surplus funds for the establishment of joint development institutions.

About the Contributors

Hussain Khallaf is member of The Arab Literary Board in Cairo, Egypt. He was formerly minister of cultural relations of the United Arab Republic (1958-61), ambassador and chief of the Egyptian delegation of the United Nations in Geneva, advisor to the League of Arab States, and professor of economics, Cairo University.

Mohamad W. Khouja is an executive with the Kuwait Real Estate Investment Corporation, Kuwait. He was formerly senior economic advisor at the Kuwait Fund for Arab Economic Development, and associate professor of economics at Oklahoma State University. He is the author of several works on economics, including *The Economy of Kuwait*.

Carlos Massad is advisor to the UN Economic Commission for Latin America (ECLA/CEPAL), Santiago, Chile, and is consultant to several international organizations of the United Nations and Inter-American Systems. He was formerly president of the Central Bank and minister of finance of Chile. He is author of numerous works on international economics.

Amaury Porto de Oliveira is consul-general of Brazil in Rotterdam, The Netherlands. He was formerly posted as a career diplomat in Caracas and in several Arab capitals. He is specializing in petroleum affairs, and is author of numerous works on international energy policy.

Alejandro Orfila is secretary general at the Organization of American States, Washington, D.C. He was formerly the Argentinian ambassador to Japan and the United States. He is receipient of several honorary doctorates in law, and is the author of several books and articles, including *The Agenda before the Americas* (1980).

Armando Prugue is manager of the Inter-American Development Bank (IDB) Staff Retirement Fund. Since 1963 he has assumed a number of positions at the IDB, including legal consultant and executive director for Argentina, Peru, and Colombia. He is the author of several books, including *Seven Years of LAFTA* (in Spanish).

Fehmy Saddy is an executive with the Olayan Group of companies, Saudi Arabia. He was formerly professor of political science at Kuwait University and American University of Beirut, Lebanon. He is the author of several works on Middle Eastern and international economics.

Abdullah H. Tarik is president of Arab Petroleum Consultants, and publisher of the authoritative periodical *Arab Oil* (in Arabic). He was the founder and first director of Oil and Mineral Affairs Department—later the Ministry of Petroleum and Mines of Saudi Arabia. He was co-founder of OPEC in 1960.

Francisco Orrego Vicuna is professor of international law and relations, and director of the Institute of International Studies of the University of Chile. He is ambassador and head of the Chilean delegation of the UN Law of the Sea Conference and to the Chilean–Argentine negotiations on the Beagle Channel. He was formerly visiting professor at Stanford University and member of the Inter-American Juridical Committee of the Organization of American States. He is author of numerous books on international law and relations.

Index

141